THIS BOOK
BELONGS TO

....

....

©COPYRIGHT
2024

The content contained within this book may not be reproduced, duplicated, or transmitted without direct written permission from the author or the publisher. Under no circumstances will any blame or legal responsibility be held against the publisher, or author, for any damages, reparation, or monetary loss due to the information contained within this book. Either directly or indirectly.

Legal Notice:
This book is copyright protected. This book is only for personal use. You cannot amend, distribute, sell, use, quote, or paraphrase any part, or the content within this book, without the consent of the author or publisher.

Disclaimer Notice:
Please note the information contained within this document is for educational and entertainment purposes only. All effort has been executed to present accurate, up-to-date, and reliable, complete information. No warranties of any kind are declared or implied. Readers acknowledge that the author is not engaging in the rendering of legal, financial, medical, or professional advice. The content within this book has been derived from various sources. Please consult a licensed professional before attempting any techniques outlined in this book. By reading this document, the reader agrees that under no circumstances is the author responsible for any losses, direct or indirect, which are incurred as a result of the use of the information contained within this document, including, but not limited to — errors, omissions, or inaccuracies.

Thank you for Purchasing my book and taking the time to read it from front to back. I am always grateful when a reader chooses my work and I hope you enjoyed it!

With the vast selection available online, I am touched that you chose to be purchasing my work and take valuable time out of your life to read it. My hope is that you feel you made the right decision.

I very much would like to know what you thought of the book. Please take the time to write an honest and informative review on Amazon.com. Your experience and opinions will be of great benefit to me and those readers looking to make an informed choice.

With much thanks.

Table of Contents

1. Why we blog — 5
2. Planning blog posts — 10
3. Establishing your blog's guardrails — 13
4. What do you mean, "never run out of ideas?" — 27
5. Capturing your ideas — 32
6. Getting blog post ideas — 40
7. Vetting your ideas — 52
8. The five filters — 58
9. Why we strategize blog posts — 83
10. Planning blog posts people want to read — 91
11. Planning for robots — 102
12. Planning for promotion — 111
13. How to outline a blog post — 116
14. Wrapping up — 135

1

WHY WE BLOG

This guide is primarily about how to plan blog posts. However, planning blog posts won't do us all that much good if we don't understand why we're blogging in the first place. So before we explore how to plan blog posts that attract customers, clients, and donors, let's take just a little bit of time to get on the same page as far as why we've begun the blogging journey.

You have plenty of reasons to blog, but they all rest on one basic assumption: **you believe you have something worthwhile to say.** Granted, this assumption fuels all communication channels, be it blog, email, direct mail, cold calls, banner ads, or sandwich boards.

So out of all the channels available, why would we choose to blog?

It's a fair question. It's easier to set up a Facebook page than it is to set up a blog. It's less time-consuming to make a phone call than it is to write a (proper) blog post. It requires less technical know-how to design a banner ad.

Come to think of it, blogging may be the most brain-intensive, slow-starting, horrifying messaging channel we use in business today. (It's that or public speaking.) So why do we do it?

We blog because, more so than any other channel, a blog gives us a place to lay a strong, evergreen foundation for the rest of our messaging.

Therefore, before we discuss how to do it well, let's explore why we should do it well.

We blog to be found

Your blog is the online magnet drawing prospective customers to your website. As you'll see later in this guide, the blog is where you will answer your audience's questions. The blog is where you will give them practical, helpful advice. The blog is where you will show potential customers just how brilliant you and your products are, and make them want nothing more than to do business with you.

Can you send these kinds of messages through other channels? Absolutely! Which leads us to the unique reason we need to blog well.

We blog well so that we can be found online.

"But," you might say, "we already have a website! Surely we can be found online already at AwesomeBrand.edu, right?"

It's true. If you have a website, then odds are good that people looking for you will find you. However, that's only going to be effective for the people who already know where they should be looking.

That's not a problem. After all, if people are specifically looking for your brand, you want them to find you. But there's a bigger group of people out there, and they're not looking for you, specifically. They're looking for solutions to the problems you solve.

Think about how you use Google. You look up solutions to problems around the house, like "How to get rid of squirrels." You look up ways to get things done at work, like, "How to get my business on Google Maps." You look up random questions that pop into your head, like, "What's the most populous city in Europe?" (As of the time I'm writing this book, it's London.)

Now, let's say you're running a business called "Awesome Gardening Tools" and you sell, well, awesome gardening tools. You don't want to stop at only reaching the people looking for your tools, specifically. You want people to find your website when they Google things like:

- "Shovel vs. spade"

- "Garden plants that don't need much sunlight"

- "Homemade weed killer"

A well-strategized and well-executed blog can make that happen. That's because blogging opens us up to reach more than just the people already looking for us. It's a tool that makes it easier to be discovered by the people we are best suited to help.

This brings us to another big concept that we'll need to address before we dive into the details of blogging: the concept of inbound marketing.

Inbound marketing

Inbound marketing started gaining popularity among marketers around 2006. At that time, most people did marketing the way it had been done for decades:

- They bought billboards

- They ran TV commercials

- They sent mass mailings

And even the digitally savvy companies were paying third party firms to send marketing emails for them (spam!) or plastering annoying banner ads anywhere on the Internet (annoying!).

That's when some marketers thought, "Wait a minute. I'm spending all my money trying to get in front of as many eyeballs as possible … but do they even *want* to see me? What if I just started creating material that drew the customers I can actually help to me?"

It was brilliant. And it introduced the world to a new kind of marketing. Instead of "spray and pray" messaging (trying to get in front of as many people as possible), people have begun focusing on getting in front of as many of the right people as possible. And instead of muscling their way in front of those ideal customers with lots of ads, people began to write and design resources that helped those people solve their problems.

At its core, the difference between outbound and inbound marketing is the difference between push and pull. Instead of spending your energy pushing as much messaging as possible, you focus on finding the ways to pull the right people in.

The main channel for marketing like this? Blogs. This is one reason so many company websites include a blog. (If you haven't noticed this already, there's no way you'll miss it now!)

Inbound marketing is determining who your ideal customers are and attracting them with content they love. Let's break that down just a bit.

• "Dream customers" are the people who would absolutely love the cool stuff you offer: your products, your services, your prices, and your values. They are those people who will brag about you to anyone who will listen.

• "Attracting" involves the whole marketing process: from the first time they hear about your brand to the time they buy.

• "Content" is the material you make for (or share with) those dream customers. It could be blog posts, emails, infographics, whitepapers, ebooks, or even speaking engagements.

Your blog is going to be where a great deal of this happens. (And the parts that don't take place on your blog will still get a lot of support from it!) You will publish content on your blog, that content will attract your dream customer.

We'll get into how this happens later in the book. For now, remember that one of the main reasons we blog is to be found—which is where the whole inbound marketing process begins.

2

PLANNING BLOG POSTS

OK, I'll admit it: planning isn't fun for everyone. Some people love it. My wife and I are those people. We'll stay up late at night making plans. We're masters of outlines and timelines and roadmaps and strategies. It's what we love.

But some people hate it. I have a lot of friends who love, love, love to cut to the chase and dive right into the work before them. They can't stand the idea of pausing—they want to get on with it already. If you're one of these folks, I envy you a little bit—especially when it comes to the stuff we'll cover in the next chapter!

Some people hate planning. Some love it. That means not everyone is super excited to read this chapter.

However, of all the sections in this book, this is by far the most important. So I'll make a promise to both groups right now.

If you love planning: Fasten your seatbelts. Even if you're the most organized person your accountant has ever met, we have a lot of new territory to cover in this chapter. We're going to look at how planning specifically relates to blogging—and as you can imagine, being a fantastic planner doesn't automatically make you a fantastic blog planner. We need to look at some pretty technical stuff: keyword research, competitive analyses, and the like. Even if you've written books on planning in general, you're going to learn a great deal in this chapter. Stay with me.

If you hate planning: I get it. You'd probably rather skip to the next chapter on writing. But trust me, if you master the art and science of planning blog posts, *you will end up writing even more than you would otherwise*. I know it sounds weird. But taking the time to plan out your blog posts actually reduces the time it takes to write top-notch pieces—which means you'll be able to produce even more content week in and week out!

At this point you might be thinking, "Jeffrey, why are you making such a big deal out of this? We get it. Planning is good."

Here's why. Remember how we briefly overviewed the blogging process at the beginning of this book? It's a three-part process:

1. Planning blog posts

2. Writing blog posts

3. Promoting blog posts

The planning piece of writing blog posts directly affects how well you can pull off the other two parts. For example, a blog post written without a strategic plan in mind may turn out to be a fantastic post. It may cover a topic with an elegance and charm that surpasses any other article in publication today. But if you didn't properly plan the article, if you didn't build it in a way that would get shared by influencers in your target audience, and if you didn't format it in a way that makes it easy for Google to find … you might be the only one who ever reads it. Conversely, a lack of planning can undermine talented promoters. Even if you have the most brilliant set of contacts, even if you have hundreds of thousands of dollars to spend on advertising, and even if your post goes million-hits-a-day viral, without strategic planning ahead of time, you're going to miss out on a lot of wins those promotion efforts could have brought in.

This is why we plan, and we plan hard. When it comes to blogging, everything hinges on planning.

In this section, we'll explore the important aspects of planning, and how to pull the process off:

1. Establishing your blog's guardrails

2. Coming up with blog post ideas

3. Vetting those ideas

4. Planning for people

5. Planning for robots

6. Planning for promotion

7. Outlines and estimates

We'll start with establishing your blog's guardrails.

3

ESTABLISHING YOUR BLOG'S GUARDRAILS

Guardrails keep us from veering off the road into trees, lakes, ravines, and espresso chalets. They don't keep us from changing lanes, and they don't limit how fast we drive. They just help us stay on the road.

We use similar methodology when we're planning out our blog posts. Setting up "guardrails" for our blog helps us decide what to blog about and what not to blog about—which will come in really handy in the chapter after the next (when we get into the nitty-gritty of vetting blog post ideas).

We're going to look at how to set up your blog's guardrails in this chapter by focusing on three main areas:

1. Your audience: whom are you writing for?

2. Your scope: what are you writing about?

3. Your stance: what do you and your audience think?

Every single blog post you publish should make sense in context of these three areas. So for this chapter, we'll look at each of these and examine some practical ways to set up your own blog guardrails.

Guardrails by your audience

The first thing to keep in mind when you're writing any kind of message is the person who will read it. This is easy for us to remember when we're thinking of personal emails, letters, and text messages, but there's something about the public, available-to-anyone nature of blogs that makes it easy to forget all about the audience.

For whatever reason, blogs often become the most introspective, self-serving, naval-gazingest parts of a brand's online presence. And when I say "brand," I'm not limiting it to organizations. Personal bloggers deal with this, too. The temptation is to blog for ourselves, and hope that our words will resonate with the right people.

Granted, that's not impossible. There is a chance that by consistently blogging about what you and your organization love, your ideal audience will stumble upon a post of yours, fall in love, and keep coming back to hear everything you say. But we're better marketers than that, right?

You'll have a better time attracting an audience if you have a good idea of whom that audience is. The better you know your readers (or your future readers), the more fine-tuned your content will be.

Now, this is normally the point in the ebook at which the author would tell you to create buyer personas. And if you've been in the marketing world very long, this is normally the point at which you're thinking, **"Audience personas? Doesn't that take a lot of research?"**

Persona research can be a huge task, and for good reason. The more thorough your persona research is, the better you'll be able to write for them. However, it's not an all-or-nothing game. I've laid out these options in order of highest to lowest in terms of price, accuracy, and value.

1. Invest in persona research

If you're a research junky who has plenty of time on your hands, or if you have the funds to hire someone to do the research for you, this is the path I recommend. You want to find the perfect match for what you're offering to the world. Find out where they live, how much money they make, what their age is, what they're interested in, who they vote for, etc.

This should be a deep-dive: you want to walk away with a crystal-clear picture of whom you're trying to reach, and how you can help them.

Of course, this is expensive, either in your own work hours or in hiring someone to do the research for you. However, it's the most enlightening, data-backed approach, too.

2. Sample your current audience

Unless you're launching a new business tomorrow, you have a few opportunities for defining your target audience at your fingertips right now: your current customers. Start by grabbing a piece of paper (or opening a new document, or a new Evernote file, or whatever suits you), and begin two separate lists.

For your first list, take down the names of the top 5 current customers at your company. These aren't necessarily the customers with the highest dollar value of orders—they're the ones who make you think, "I wish I could get a hundred more customers like you!" Take down a list of the ones you'd hate to see close their accounts—the customers you'll always brag about.

Now, look at that list. What are some common themes? What are their industries? What are your contacts' positions? What audiences do they serve? Where are they located? Why did they choose you? How do you help them? If you were to sort them into groups of two or more, how would you sort them?

Congratulations: you've created a few persona sketches. If you want to get some more information, you could create a brief survey for your current star customers. If a survey seems too formal, you can always invite people to lunch and prepare a few questions ahead of time.

This isn't as research-backed as a full-on persona research project is, but at least you get some intel on the kind of people you want to attract.

But what if you don't have this luxury? Well, there's another option I'd recommend.

3. Write for one person you know

This is the bootstrapper's approach to persona building. If you don't have the time, energy, or resources to invest in persona research or sampling your current audience, you can always try this:

Think of one person you know whom you'd like to become a customer or client. Then write to that person.

Is it scientifically data-backed? Nope. Is it extensive? Nope. Is it going to leave a lot of opportunity on the table? You bet. But it's also the least expensive, least time-consuming, and—dare I say it?—the easiest way to start writing.

Picture one person, and it can't be an imaginary person. It needs to be a real-life person whom you've had a real-life conversation with. Think of the questions they have, the challenges they face, and the goals they're striving toward.

Now write for that person.

You might ask, "OK, I see how cost-effective this can be, but does it work?"

Put it this way: if it weren't for this approach, you wouldn't be reading this book.

You see, my blogging really took off when I used this method. I didn't have money. I didn't have time to do research. And I didn't have a current audience to interview. When I started my first blog, I had zero readers who weren't married to me. But I had an idea of who should read it! I was writing this blog (focused on Bible literacy) with a particular friend of mine in mind—and I wrote every post with him in mind for the next 6 months in the hopes of attracting more people who wanted similar content. And if it hadn't been for the success of that site, I wouldn't have started my company, and I wouldn't be writing this book.

Would I recommend this as a long-term strategy for determining your readership? NO WAY. Writing for that one friend was great, but my target audience has shifted since then. You will want to invest in a more sophisticated approach to market research later on. But this is far, far, far better than nothing.

So what?

If you try any of these tactics, you'll leave with a target audience in mind. This will function as a guardrail for your blog as you think up new blog post ideas, vet them, and strategize them (all of which we'll cover in this section of the book).

But audience is just one thing to keep in mind. Now let's look at another important piece of the puzzle: scope.

Guardrails by scope

Knowing your audience is a good thing, but it's not the only thing that will keep your blog in line. You've asked the question, "Who's reading my blog?" Now it's time to ask, "What am I writing about?"

This may sound like a really dumb question with a number of obvious answers. "I'll write about whatever interests my audience." "I'll write about what's happening in our corporate culture." "I'll write about why people should buy our product." "I'll write about deadlines for limited-time discounts."

You could write about any of these things. They're not necessarily bad subject matter if done in the right voice (which we'll cover next).

However, if you're going to keep a consistent blog that both resonates with your audience and keeps them coming back for more, you're going to need better answers that these. A good blog is both for some*one* and about some*thing*. You need to know your audience and your scope so you can consistently deliver the right blog posts.

Consistency is key here. Remember the reason why we're blogging in the first place: we blog to be found. And we strive to blog in such a way that when we're found, the visitors will come back for more. How do we do that?

We do so by being consistent in what we blog about. When I put it this way, it sounds a little abstract, so let's try a more concrete example.

Suppose you go to a conference and hear an insightful message from one of the speakers on the topic of the U.S. economy. You are so impressed by her talk that you look her up on Google and find her website. The latest article on her website shows the rise and fall of the U.S. Dollar's value over the past 200 years, and you think, "Wow, this lady really has a way of bringing such a boring topic to life!" So you bookmark her website.

But then strange things start to happen. You go to her site a week later in hopes of seeing another article on economics, but instead you see a bunch of pictures from her latest trip to Paris. "That's weird," you think, "I thought she was an expert on economics. But I guess everyone needs a vacation sometime. I'll just check back later." Now, imagine you're among the tiny percentage of readers who actually checks back later (most readers don't!). Imagine you come back to her site the next week and see an article listing 10 things she loves about driving a hybrid car.

Would you still think of this person as an expert on economics? Maybe. But would you come back to her blog for thoughts on economics? No! Why would you waste your time going to a site that just might post an economics article once or twice a year?

Now, let's look at this fictitious example in the context of consistency. This blogger had you as a fan, but lost you because her messaging was inconsistent. She hadn't defined the scope of her blog, and because of that, you're no longer interested in reading what she writes.

That's why it's so important to not only think of your audience, but also think of your scope. You need a good idea of what subject matter you will cover on your blog. But it doesn't stop with you: your readers need to know what subject matter you cover, too.

You're in a good spot if, when someone asks you, "What do you blog about?" you can give a one-sentence answer without hesitation. You're in an amazing spot if, when someone asks your readers, "What does this company blog about?" they can give the same answer.

So, how do we get there? The first step is to set up your blog's scope. There are a few ways of doing this.

1. Go broad

One way you can set your scope is by determining to keep it very, very general. You can have a few personas in mind and then write whatever content you think may possibly appeal to them. There are some sites that can pull this off, but they're mostly news sites with lots of writers and editors working around the clock to pump out as much content as possible.

This approach has a few benefits, the obvious being broad appeal and low chances of going off-base. A broad scope can draw in a lot of readers, and possibly a lot of leads. However, it comes with some pretty obvious problems, too.

The main difficulty here with this approach is that the broader your scope, the smaller percentage of your readership will be interested in what you offer. You might publish posts that are seen by 10 million readers every month, but that may not do you much good if only 10 of those readers could ever become customers.

Another issue with this approach is the kind of investment you need to put into it. Churning out mass-appeal content can be exhausting:

and you need to put out a lot of it if you want to avoid looking inconsistent. Remember: if a site publishes 100 articles on 100 topics every day, it's a news site; if a site publishes 100 articles on 100 topics over three years, it's an inconsistent site.

You can probably tell that, for the most part, I'm biased against this approach for most companies. You probably can't support this approach with enough content to make it attract a large amount of leads, and even if you did, you probably can't support the process of weeding out the duds.

2. Only talk about your offerings

We've looked at one extreme; it's time to examine the other. While some organizations choose to go very broad, others take the opposite approach: they only talk about their own brands.

Of the two approaches we've looked at, this is by far the more common. A lot of brands have a "News" section of their website where they post updates about what's happening. Common posts include:

• Photos from the last company picnic

• Announcements of prominent product updates (this is especially common in the software world)

• Promotion and discount deadlines

The upside of posts like these: only people who are already very, very interested in your brand will read them. The downside: that's a pretty narrow slice of the total population you could reach on your blog. This probably isn't a surprise to you if you're reading this guide.

This is a common struggle that organizations of all kinds face. When we blog, we're always tempted to write for ourselves. (We touched on this earlier when we were discussing audiences.) And writing for ourselves tends to manifest in two major ways:

• We blog about what we're doing.

• We blog about what we want people to do.

This is just human nature: we care about ourselves. That means that of all the blog topics in the universe, these will always be the easiest things for us to write about. We'll always have something to say about what we're doing, and there will always be more things we want other people to do. It's easy to blog about what's on our minds, and we're all really good at thinking about ourselves.

Here's the problem: **everyone else cares about themselves, too.** Every potential customer is more interested in how to improve his life than he is interested in your corporate 5k run. Every decision-maker is more interested in reaching this quarter's strategic goals than she is interested in meeting your office dog. (That doesn't mean they don't want to know about you. It just means you're not the priority: they are!)

That's why our job as communicators is so challenging: we need to reach our audiences in ways that resonate with them while meeting our business goals. Which is why I (and most content marketing experts) would encourage you to blog between the extremes of these last two options. This is what I call the Two Rings Out Rule.

3. The Two Rings Out Rule

Instead of limiting your scope to your own operations, instead of setting your scope at nigh-unachievable "mass appeal," I recommend setting your scope just beyond the audience you're currently attracting. I call this the Two Rings Out Rule, and here's how it works.

Start with what you can offer. It might be the world's most comfortable hiking boots. It might be the most durable windbreakers on the market. Make a brief list of the things you can do better than anyone else.

Now, think about your audience. Why do they want what you have to offer? Make a list of key desires you can satisfy. This isn't an easy exercise. For example, let's say you're on the marketing staff at a private university:

• Students who want an urban campus don't just want an urban campus. They might want to feel like they're living in a big city. They might want to be walking distance from the city's best pizza, coffee, and bowling alleys. Think about the reasons they might want to go to a school in the city instead of a green, rural campus. (Hint: ask them directly!)

• Students who want a strong athletic program don't just want a strong athletic program. They might want to make the most of their younger years by playing the games they love as much as possible. They might want to hear the roar of an entire student body chanting their name after scoring a touchdown. They might want to make Mom and Dad proud.

Tough, right? These questions will take a while to answer: you'll need to use every ounce of imagination and empathy you can muster. But when you're done, you will have a list of persona desires your brand can satisfy like no other brand can.

But we're not done yet. Now that you have a list of desires you can satisfy, it's time to think about the categories those desires fall into. Going back to the university example, if your list of persona desires looked like this:

• Being able to access the most beautiful hikes

- Being mentored by experienced businessmen

- Becoming a success story for my family (or hometown)

- Seeing more of the world

A few themes stand out: outdoor exploration and entrepreneurship.

Now, you would blog about these topics to your target audience. This keeps your scope focused on both your audience and your business goals.

I call this the **Two Rings Out Rule** because I like to think of it as a way to stretch outside of what I'm naturally inclined to write. I think of three concentric rings:

1. The center ring contains all the self-serving content I want to write about my own brand. In the university case, this would include messages like, "Apply now," or "Request information," and "Check out our programs."

2. The first ring out contains the content bridging the gap between me and my target audience. This includes messages like, "What if you could walk from class to an authentic English tea room?"

3. The second ring out contains the content the target audience is already interested in consuming. This could include posts like, "The top 10 hikes in the continental United States," or, "25 millionaires teaching teenagers how to become millionaires too"—a killer way to plug one or two of your business faculty, by the way.

You want to set the scope of your blog two rings out! That's how you can generate content that resonates with your personas and pulls them in.

"But Jeffrey, how are we going to pull people from two rings out to that center ring of getting them to do what we want them to do?"

We'll get to that when we discuss the last part of every blog post: the call to action. That's where you'll relate the blog post to your own business objectives in a way that makes sense to your audience.

Guardrails by stance

There's one more important guardrail to keep in mind as you plan out blog posts: your stance.

This one's pretty obvious, so we won't spend too much time on it here. There aren't many times that you will find yourself blogging something you don't believe. There aren't many times you will have to ask yourself, "Is this blog post going to help me or hurt me?" But it's still an important factor to consider, especially when it comes to guest posting.

Yes, guest posting. Not all of your blog content will live on your own blog, and not all of the content on your blog will be yours! One of the best ways to build relationships with the influencers your target audience looks up to is by guest posting, which usually manifests as one of the following:

1. Influencers posting content you wrote on their blogs

2. You posting content that influencers wrote on your blog

3. Collaborative works by you and those influencers

In any of these cases, it's very important that whatever you're writing is aligned with your brand's general beliefs, philosophy, and mission.

Of course, this expands beyond just the realm of guest posting. If your blog comments on events in your community, you will want to make sure your commentary aligns with your brand. If your blog discusses politics or religious preferences, make sure you're doing so in a way that reinforces your brand's stance.

Recap

We've looked at three main guardrails you will want to set for your blog: your audience, your scope, and your stance. We discussed these first because, if you keep these in mind, you will find the rest of this section on planning blog posts will be a much easier, more fruitful read.

One important note before we move on: **your guardrails are not static.** Your audience, scope, and stance may shift over time—and when it does, you will want to keep those shifts in mind as you plan even newer content. I would recommend revisiting these guardrails at least every two years with your marketing, sales, and communication teams to make sure your blogging efforts are on target.

OK. Now that we've set up our blog guardrails, let's get into some fun stuff. In the next chapter, we'll look at how to get ideas for blog posts—this is one of my favorite parts of the blogging process, so I'm looking forward to discussing it with you!

4

WHAT DO YOU MEAN, "NEVER RUN OUT OF IDEAS?"

The crushing void.

That's what an empty blog feels like. You know you need to write something—in fact, you need to write a lot of somethings! But what are you going to write? How do you make the leap from not blogging at all to consistently publishing new thoughts online? Where will those ideas come from? And how do you know if those ideas are any good?

This crushing void is one of the biggest difficulties people face when they begin a blog. Even if you've already been blogging for a while, you remember the feeling. And that feeling doesn't always go away after you've been blogging for a while. We hit dry spells: periods of time when blog post ideas just don't flow as freely as they used to. What happens then?

The next two chapters are going to tackle this problem. First, we'll look at ways to come up with ideas—and never run out of them! And in the following chapter, we'll examine ways to make sure only the best ideas see the light of day on our blogs.

"Never run out of ideas?" That might sound like a big promise to make. I can understand why. Ideas don't come easy to everyone, and ideas on things to write are even tougher to come by. But I think the difficulty most of us face when we begin blogging (or when we start trying to blog well) stems from two core problems in our thinking.

Problem #1: we try to get and vet ideas at the same time

The first problem is that we assume that, when we're coming up with ideas, they need to be good ideas. I've been blogging for about three years now, and I can tell you right now that this assumption does us more harm than good. I crippled myself in my early days as a blogger by trying to come up with winning blog post ideas, and only winning blog post ideas. The result? I not only talked myself out of bad ideas, I set myself up to doubt that I would come up with good ideas at all.

You can see how counterproductive this is! Instead of allowing myself to come up with many, many ideas and then choose the best, I thought every idea was either golden or garbage. And guess what? A lot of ideas are garbage. But sometimes you need to come up with 19 garbage ideas before you get one golden idea.

This is why I've intentionally split up the process of getting ideas and the process of vetting ideas into two separate chapters. They're two separate processes, and the better we can separate them, the better we'll get at both!

But this is just one of the core problems that stand in our way of coming up with great blog ideas. The other one doesn't have such a simple solution.

Problem #2: we don't practice ideation

Ideation is a skill. Sure, some people are naturally better at it than others. In fact, ideation is one of Gallup's StrengthsFinders strengths (and it's one that both my wife and I have in our top five strengths). But that doesn't mean that the skill of ideation is specific to only those who are naturally gifted in that area. Anyone can ideate if they practice.

That's why this chapter is chock-full of actionable ideation assignments. This chapter will help you work out the idea-generating part of your brain. It will be slow progress at first, but soon you'll find yourself coming up with idea after idea after idea.

I like to think of ideation as a skill similar to working an espresso bar. I worked at a coffee shop when I was a teenager. And this wasn't a laid-back hipster café where people wanted to stop by, enjoy a pourover, and read half a novel. No, this was a drive-thru coffee shop at a shopping center in Raleigh, North Carolina. It was busy. People wanted their coffee right away—they were on their way to work, soccer practice, etc.

And there I was, seventeen years old, first day on the espresso bar, trying to figure out how the blazes to keep the drinks coming. I had to steam enough milk to make five different drinks in a row. I had to remember all the drink recipes. I had to keep track of all the custom orders with extra shots, flavor substitutions, skim milk, soy milk, organic milk, yada, yada, yada. I was slow. Customers got angry.

I was finishing my shift when my coworker Andy asked how my first day on the espresso bar was.

"Terrible. I don't know how you guys do this every day," I said.

Andy nodded, and said, "We've all been there. And then we weren't. I don't know how to explain it, but one day you'll walk in, start making drinks, and wonder how you ever struggled with this."

I must have looked doubtful, because then he said, "Trust me."

And Andy was right. I struggled through making beverages for about five weeks. Then one day, it was easy. I had practiced and practiced and practiced until half of the job had become muscle memory. I went from the kid who took forever to make five drinks to the kid who could make ten drinks at a time. Instead of people waiting by the coffee bar for me to finish their order, I would have their cappuccinos ready for them by the time they had made it to the cash register.

I'm not saying this because I need you to think I'm a great barista. (I've lost about 90% of those skills to complete lack of practice—and my sister is twice the barista I ever was!) I'm saying this because coming up with blog ideas takes a lot of practice. But once you've worked out that part of your brain, you'll find yourself pumping out blog ideas all day, every day. You will wonder how you ever struggled with it!

Moving on

We've looked at two major problems in our thinking that we have when it comes to coming up with blog ideas:

1. We try to get and vet ideas simultaneously.

2. We don't practice ideation.

If you've never struggled with either of these problems, thanks for putting up with me thus far. You may wonder if the material we've covered applies to you. I think it does, and here's why: even if you don't have these issues, the people you work with do. You might be the person they need to help them undo these ways of thinking—

which will lead to more awesome, team-generated blog ideas to work with!

So now that we're all on the same page, let's look at some practical ways to generate ideas.

5

CAPTURING YOUR IDEAS

The first step in generating ideas might sound a little counterintuitive. We're not going to start with sources of ideas or mental exercises or inspirational quotes from Thomas Edison. In fact, we're not going to start by creating any ideas at all.

We're going to start by giving our ideas a place to live.

We start here because even if you're coming up with thousands of awesome ideas a day, you can't execute on them all. And unless you have an eidetic memory, most of those ideas are going to disappear come tomorrow. Call me an idea miser, but that just seems like a waste. Plus, we've already established that ideation takes practice. That means these ideas don't come easy. You're putting in a lot of work to come up with all these ideas—it would be a shame to see them lost to something as mundane as a regular memory or momentary distraction.

That's why we first want to give our ideas a place to land. We need to get them out of our heads and into something a little better at storing ideas. You can call this place whatever you like, and there are a variety of tools you can use to create such a place. But as for me, I call it a content well.

I call it a content well because, if we commit to capturing our ideas, this place will be a bottomless, never-ending source of blog material. It's the well we can always go back to, throw in a bucket, and pull out something to write.

And once you've got the hang of managing a content well, you'll start to see three very, very powerful benefits of having one:

1. You'll make vetting ideas a lot easier

We've already discussed a little bit how getting ideas and vetting ideas are two separate processes. When you develop a content well, you make it a lot easier to keep those processes separate. You can chuck as many ideas into the content well as you want, and then when you're ready to vet your ideas, you have plenty of ideas to sift through.

2. You'll make writing posts a lot easier

Just like having a content well helps us separate getting ideas from vetting ideas, it also helps us isolate the writing process. If you vet your ideas well and strategize your posts well (which we'll get to in a couple of chapters), you will be able to sit down and write.

This is important, because the state of mind that's best for planning posts is different from the state of mind that's best for writing posts. I learned this the hard way. I used to write posts by toggling back and forth between planning out a post, writing it, and then getting an idea for another post right in the middle of writing. I wasn't keeping a very good content well at this time, so I'd immediately stop writing the post I was working on and start planning around the new idea. Once that was planned out, I would try to get back to work on my original post. But could I concentrate? Nope—my brain was in planning mode, and I had to work hard to get back into writing mode. That took time and energy, and the result was that I could take days to write a single blog post.

(If it takes you days or more to write a blog post, take heart—I'll show you how to trim down the writing time in the next section of the book on producing content.)

But then I started maintaining a content well. It changed everything, and has given me two advantages in terms of writing. First, I can block out time to write, sit down, and know exactly what I am supposed to work on. Second, when I'm interrupted by new post ideas, I can quickly dump them into the content well and get back to work. What used to be a huge distraction (sometimes eating up more than an hour at a time) now takes me about 30 seconds. A new idea is a milder distraction than getting a coffee refill, going to the bathroom, or standing up to stretch. All because I gave my ideas a place to land!

3. You won't lose track of your ideas.

This is an obvious benefit, right? If your ideas have a place to live, you don't need to depend on your memory to keep track of them all.

But enough about how awesome content wells are. Let's get practical.

How to make a content well

Making a content well is a two-step process: choosing your tools and organizing them for use.

Step 1: Choosing your tools

Good content wells come in many forms, but they will all have these traits in common:

Good content wells are easy to access at any time.

This is vital. Ideas are hard to tame; they will strike at any time, and you want to capture them as soon as possible. That means your content well needs to be immediately accessible. The system I use has a mobile app on my phone, so it's incredibly easy to log new ideas as they hit me. (Well, unless I'm in the shower.)

You might use a pad and paper. You might use a note-taking app. You might use a project management tool (which I'll show you in just a moment). It just needs to be available to you whenever ideas strike, which is why I strongly discourage letting your content well live exclusively on a work computer or work-related account.

Good content wells aren't public.

If your ideas are on display to others, you will censor yourself. Remember: getting ideas and vetting ideas are separate processes! If you know anyone you want to impress (or anyone you're afraid of disappointing) is looking at your ideas, you're setting yourself up to have a really shallow content well.

Does this mean you keep your ideas secret? Not necessarily. For example, my wife and I share a content well for each of our blogs. She's not afraid of me shooting down ideas before it's time to vet them, and vice versa. I also share my content wells with clients and coworkers when I'm collaborating on content marketing projects. Bottom line: share your content well with people you trust—people who won't judge you for coming up with crazy ideas, so long as you vet the bad ones out later.

Good content wells are easy to change.

You're going to move ideas around a lot as you vet and strategize and write posts. You want a solution that can handle the volatile process of ideation. This is why I don't recommend using tattoos on your left arm as your content well.

Good content wells are easy to search.

You don't need a content well to be set up with Google-esque querying capabilities, but you do need an easy way to find ideas you've had in the past. After all, you've created this well as a place to find your ideas long after you've put them out of your mind. It would be a shame if you couldn't find those ideas when you needed them!

You might use a spreadsheet, or you might use different tabs in your notebook, or you might use a digital sorting and labeling method. Whatever works for you—just so long as you don't lose your ideas in your content well.

My recommendation: Trello

This tool does all of these with excellence. And it's free. Just to be clear, I don't get any kickbacks from Trello for saying this. I've tried several methods: pencil and notebook, spreadsheet, word processing document, etc. They all work. I'm not knocking any of these methods, but Trello has been the very best fit for me. Here's what a sample content well of mine looks like in Trello:

If you're already familiar with Trello, you know where I'm going with this. It's a solution that meets the criteria of a great content well described above:

1. It's easy to access. I can dump ideas into that first column on the left all I want. And since I have the Trello app on my phone, I can throw ideas in here as they come to me.

2. It's not public. I can decide who sees it and who doesn't.

3. It's easy to change. I can drag any of these ideas to another column without needing to rewrite anything. It's super simple.

4. It's easy to search. This is a very, very basic sample I've included here. But I can label different ideas, search by categories, and sort those columns. It's very easy to find exactly what I need.

You probably noticed all those columns and are wondering what they're all about. Fair enough—that's next on the agenda.

Once you've chosen your tools, you need to organize them in a way that makes sense for future use.

Step 2: Organizing your content well

You'll be happy to know that this part of the process is a lot simpler than choosing your tools! There are many ways you can organize your content well, but because different brands publish different content within different guardrails, I'm just going to stick with the essentials here.

You need a place for unvetted ideas.

In the example Trello board I mention above, this is the "Ideas" column on the far left. This is where "anything goes," so to speak.

It's the brainstorm bucket of the content well—you'll dump all your ideas here so you can come back to vet them later.

You need a place for vetted ideas.

Once an idea makes the cut, you need a way to mark it as ready to start working on. When I'm working with a content well, I have a "Strategize" column immediately to the right of the "Ideas" column. This is because the next step after vetting a post idea is to start planning out what that post will look like. Moving it from the idea column saves me the time it would otherwise take me to hunt down an idea I've already approved.

You need a place to outline blog posts.

When an idea is vetted, you will then form a detailed outline of what that post will look like (which we will cover in chapter 8). This is important because when it comes time to write a blog post, you want to be able to go to your content well, pull up the next post in queue, and be able to start writing. In my content wells, I write my post outlines on the ideas in the "Strategize" card.

You need a place for blog posts that are ready to be written.

Once you've got the idea, vetted the idea, and strategized the post, you need to put it someplace where you know it's ready for you to start writing it. This is why I have a "Ready to start" column to the right of the "Strategize" column in my content wells. It lets me know how many post ideas I have in the hopper, just waiting for me to turn them into blog posts.

Building out your content well

The criteria listed above are just the essentials.

There are plenty of ways to further build out your content well. You can tag different ideas by persona, by topic, and by format. You can put due dates on ideas once they're vetted. You can assign ideas to teammates. There are plenty of ways to make this system work well for your specific brand. I've just kept to the essentials so you can get a good start without getting bogged down in the minutia of setting up a system that might not even be right for you.

Moving on

Now that we've set up a place for our ideas to live, let's look at how to come up with those ideas!

6

GETTING BLOG POST IDEAS

This is the fun part! Whether you're a natural-born idea-generator or you're just getting your feet wet in the ideation world, I think you're going to like the ground we're about to cover. That's because you're already surrounded by ideas for blog posts—in fact, we're surrounded by six idea goldmines hiding in plain sight.

Those idea sources are:

- Your own experiences

- Your friends

- Your customers

- Your competitors

- The online community

- Your own content

I'm going to drill into exactly how to get blog post ideas from each of these sources. However, there's something we need to cover before we get into those specifics: technique.

Laura, my wife and business partner, is an excellent composer, pianist, and vocalist. (And to be fair, that's what she was known as long before I knew her—that's not just nice-husbandese.) One day I had the privilege of meeting her high school vocal coach. We chatted about more than just music, but she said something that stuck with me. She said, "I don't work on people's voices. I work on their technique."

The line stuck with me because the principle isn't limited to the field of music. When it comes to blogging, you can bring any kind of experience, vocabulary, writing style, and subject matter to the table —but your technique is what really matters. And when it comes to getting blog post ideas, there's a technique that works really well for me that I'd like to share with you.

The technique: listening for questions.

A good blog post should meet some need that someone in your audience has, and I've found that many of those needs are expressed through questions. Therefore, my technique for coming up with new blog post ideas is to listen for questions that people in my audience have.

Did you notice that I wrote about "questions they have" rather than "questions they ask"? That's because most of the time we think of questions as things that are explicitly asked of us. "How much does it cost?" "What services do you offer?" "When's the deadline for registration?" However, that's not how we deal with our own questions, is it? No. We hold back.

If you've spent any time in a classroom, you know this first hand. At the end of the class, the teacher asks, "Any questions?"

What happens? Does anyone have any questions? Usually not—you and the rest of the students are ready to leave as soon as you can. And when that one student does have a question, everyone rolls their eyes and silently cries, "Why? Why? We were so close to getting out of here!"

We have all kinds of reasons for not asking questions. We don't want to take up other people's time. We don't want to look foolish. We figure we can Google them later. We dismiss them as unimportant. Whatever the reason, we don't voice every question we have, and often hold back the ones that we're most curious about.

That's why this blogging technique is about listening for questions that people aren't directly asking. When you can tap into those deep, unspoken questions, you will find yourself with an endless stream of blog ideas. And when you provide the answers to these questions, that's when your blog starts taking off.

All of this probably sounds a bit abstract, so let's go over a few practical ways to listen for questions before we talk about getting blog ideas from those sources I listed earlier.

How to listen for questions:

• Start with the obvious: take down the explicit questions.

• Pay attention to what frustrates people. They're telling you they have a problem—maybe you can write the answer.

• Note any questions you ask that others don't have an answer to. You've just created a question and shared it with them—now's your opportunity to find and share the answer.

• Listen for contrasts and comparisons. There's a wealth of questions hiding behind "this vs. that" statements and conversations.

This is not an exhaustive list of ways to listen for questions by any means, but it will get you on the right track.

The technique isn't easy, and it takes a lot of practice. You don't need to perfect it before you start collecting blog post ideas. (I certainly haven't perfected it yet.) Just keep working at it as you keep coming up with ideas. It has become a fantastic way for me to mine blog post ideas hour by hour from the six sources I mentioned above.

Speaking of which, let's start looking at how to tap those sources, shall we?

Ideas from your own experience

Start with what you know. Have you ever been in your audience's shoes? What was it like? What was most confusing to you? Which parts were the most frustrating for you? Which parts were the best? If you could go back and give yourself any advice, what would it be?

As you can see, this is a fantastic way to come up with blog post ideas. In fact, let's try an example right now. I attended an urban university in Tennessee; now let's imagine what it would be like if I were blogging for a similar school. Just by drawing from my own experience, I could write any one of these blog posts for prospective students:

- 20 advantages of going to an urban college

- You're accepted. Now what?

- City or country college? The pros and cons of each

- Which state should you go to college in?

And this list could be a lot longer.

Personal experience works well when you're part of (or were once part of) your target audience. But you may not have ever been in your target audience. What about then?

For example, let's say that instead of blogging for an urban university, I was blogging for a technical college targeting fortysomething women. At first glance, it would seem I don't have very much shared experience with this audience. Could I still pull blog post ideas from my own experience? I think so. Here are a few ideas that come to mind:

- How applying for technical college is different from applying for university

- How old are your classmates? A breakdown by school type

- 5 reasons you were smart to wait until now to get your degree

And I think you could do the same in a similar situation. Just ask yourself, "What were the biggest challenges I faced?" or, "If I were the reader, what are some of the biggest obstacles in my way?"

This is just one source of blog ideas, and it is probably the one you'll come to most. But let's move on to another really helpful source of blog post ideas: your friends.

Ideas from your friends

This one is a little sneaky.

I don't know about you, but most of my friends and family are not director- or executive-level leaders in higher education. In fact, a good amount of my friends don't even have bachelors' degrees. However, I draw blog post ideas from them all the time—and you can mine ideas from your friends and family, too.

That's because these folks have a weird way of not knowing what we do. It's odd. You can be friends with someone for ten years and they'll only have a general idea of what you do for a living (and it might not go beyond knowing your employer and job title).

For a while, this annoyed me. Then I realized two things—one was kind of sad, and the other was awesome:

1. I do the same thing to them. I assume that because I know them, I know what they do. I'm just as much of a jerk. (This is the sad one.)

2. My friends may not know much about what I do, but they are comfortable enough with me to ask questions about it. That means they might bring up questions that I'd never think to answer.

It was an odd, eye-opening experience. My friends are giving me a chance to articulate what I do and why I do it—and there's no risk of me losing a sale by thinking out loud.

So next time you're talking with your family and the conversation turns to work, pay attention to the questions they're asking (even if you think they should know the answers by now). Note their misperceptions. Learn as much as you can about their impressions of your brand. You'll get plenty of ideas to throw into your content well.

And if you're friends with a lot of people in your target market, well, you're in for a treat!

Ideas from your customers

This one should be obvious, right? If you're going to attract more customers by writing helpful blog articles, you may want to see what your current customers need (or needed) help with. There are a few ways you can do this.

- Ask them directly. Take them out for lunch or give them a call, and ask them why they chose you. Ask them what the hardest part about choosing a [whatever you provide] was. Ask them what their end goals are and how you're helping them get there. You can turn a lot of their responses into blog post ideas.

- Talk to your sales team. What were some of the most common objections leads have when considering your brand? What was the number one reason leads didn't follow through with a sale? Where do the customers come from? What's their background? This can help refine the way you perceive your audience, but it will also give you some ideas for blog posts that attract higher-quality prospects and help the duds weed themselves out.

- If you're not doing this already, create a customer feedback survey. Find out what customers enjoyed most about interacting with you, what they didn't like, why they chose you in the first place, what they wish they'd known beforehand, and what their plans for the future are. This is not to intimidate your customers—so keep the survey short. This will give you plenty (and I mean PLENTY) of ideas for your blog.

This is one of the very best sources of ideas, because you're getting content ideas directly from the kind of people you want to attract. Plus, you're leveraging your existing audience to attract an even larger one—which in my opinion, is a smart thing to do.

Ideas from your competitors

I probably shouldn't have to say this, but just to be on the safe side: this isn't about stealing ideas from competitors. There are, however, plenty of ethical ways to get blog post ideas from watching your competitors.

"Hold on. Why do we even want to do this? Aren't we supposed to be different from our competitors?" You bet. And one of the best ways to set yourself apart is by knowing exactly where the competition stands.

For example: open a Web browser and go to your website. Find the page where you list your core values. Now open another tab and do the same for your main competitor. Is there any overlap? Where do you differ? Why do you differ on these? What can you, with your values and products, offer your audience that your competitor cannot?

Bottom line: find out what sets you apart from your competition. Then throw each of those differences into the content well.

Ideas from the online community

"Online community," doesn't necessarily mean "Facebook and Twitter." There's a bit of confusion when it comes to social media from a marketing standpoint, so let's draw one distinction before we look at how to get ideas from this source: **medium is not the same as community.**

For example, let's say you're a brewery trying to reach single women in Washington State. A good deal of your prospects are on

Facebook, but they're not on Facebook to visit your page. Many of your prospects tweet, but they're not on Twitter for you. They're on Instagram, but they're not there to see your pictures.

Is it because they hate you? Not at all! It's because they've found interactive communities of people, and those communities aren't built around you. They're built around what's funny, frustrating, and interesting in your prospects' lives. Facebook is a medium, not a community. The communities spend some of their time on Facebook (and the same community engages across different social media platforms).

I like to think of social networks the way I think of malls. A mall is a place where groups of young people get together, discover products they like, and generally have fun. Some groups are going to go to Kohls. Some are going to Hot Topic. Some are going to hang out in the food court. (Me? I just want to go to the pet store.) The point is: you have different groups going to several different shops for different reasons. That's what social networks are like. *Everyone* is on social media, and they interact within different subcultures for different reasons. It's your job to figure out what your audience is using social media for—and that's where your blog post ideas will come from.

Oh, and by the way, the online community is a lot bigger than the major social networks you've heard of. When I say "online community," I include forums, subreddits, influential blogs, and things like this. It's far, far bigger than Facebook.

And of course, the social scene is always changing.

"Wait. So if it's so nebulous, how am I supposed to get any good ideas from this source?" Right. Let's look at some practical ways to figure out where your audience's online communities are and how to use that information to come up with blog post ideas.

Start by finding bloggers. Remember that list of categories we created back when we were setting up guardrails by audience? Let's put some of that to work for us. Google "[CATEGORY] blog" and see what comes up. Click through the first 10 results and see which sites come up. Ta-da! You've started your list of bloggers.

Why is this important? Because if these categories really are interesting to your prospective customers, there's a good chance some of that audience is already reading these blogs. Browse their site (or use a tool like Buzzsumo) to get an idea of what they blog about. Read their posts.

Now, is there anything you disagree with? Is there anything that could use some more explanation? Anything that could be said in a more friendly way for your target audience? Congratulations! You've come up with some blog post ideas.

Now find some Twitter communities. Most of those bloggers are probably on Twitter. Find their Twitter feeds, and then look at who's following those bloggers. Do any of their followers seem like they're in your target audience? If so, look at what they've tweeted recently. You're getting an idea of what they think is awesome, frustrating, and funny. This should give you some blog post ideas.

You're probably getting the idea. Follow your audience around online and see where they take you. At every turn, you'll either find more ways to explore their online community, more blog post ideas, or both.

Ideas from your own content

This one is a lot of fun, and it's simple. As you blog, pay attention to which posts attract the most traffic, the most social shares, the most comments, etc. Then ask, "How can I give the audience more of what they like?"

This is where I like to share what I call the Theory of Telescopic Content:

The Theory of Telescopic Content: Any piece of content can be expanded, elaborated on, or grouped with similar pieces to produce a new, helpful piece of content—which can also be expanded, elaborated on, or grouped with similar pieces to produce a new, helpful piece of content—which can also be …

For example, let's say you're a real estate agent and you write a blog post entitled, "10 steps to buying a home in Missouri." It resonates. People share it on Facebook. They comment on the post, expressing their thanks in all caps and many, many exclamation points. The post gets 5,000 views in its first 24 hours. You schedule 200 new home viewings! It's clearly something your audience loves. Now what?

The first thing I would do is write 10 step-by-step, in-depth articles on how to execute each and every one of those 10 steps. Include examples. Pull in screen shots of websites they'd need to visit. Hold your reader's hand through each step's process. Boom: you've just pulled 10 ideas out of one post!

This is one of my favorite ways to get blog post ideas, because I can use the data from my blog to inform my decisions on what posts to write next.

(By the way, it really, really helps to have Google Analytics set up on your blog if you're going to try this approach. This tool lets you see which pages on your blog people visit most, so you're not blindly guessing which posts get the most views. When it comes to measuring which posts have the most social shares, I suggest using Buzzsumo—you can just type in your blog's URL and get a report on which posts have been shared the most.)

Ready to vet?

We've covered a lot of idea-generation ground here! Now that you've set up a content well and have plenty of ideas coming in, let's shift gears and look at how to choose the right ones for your blog.

7

VETTING YOUR IDEAS

For many, the last chapter covered the hardest part of blogging: just figuring out what to blog about. But now you have a content well that you're filling with ideas. You're golden! The hard part's done! There's nothing stopping you from writing a killer blog now … right?

Not really.

In an ideal world, once we had a post idea, we could hammer that sucker out in an hour, post it at exactly the right time on the right day, and watch the traffic come a-rolling in. We don't live in that world, though. That almost never happens. For every blog post, you'll need to invest the time to plan, write, and promote it. And since your time is valuable, you want to spend it on the right ideas. You need to weed out the duds before you spend any time on them.

That's where vetting blog ideas comes in. In the last chapter, we looked at how to make a content well and how to keep it filled up. In this chapter, we'll look at what to do with the ideas you're throwing into your content well—specifically, which ideas should make it into the next phase (making an outline) and which ideas should die.

Before we jump into how we do this, we should take a moment to set a few expectations. You might be reading this part and thinking, "Oh, thanks, Jeffrey. You've just busted up my creativity blocks in the last chapter and I'm finally comfortable with coming up with new ideas—now you're going to teach me how to tear myself down again?"

It's a fair point to make, which is why we need to get an idea of where I'm going in this chapter. After all, you don't want to vet ideas in such a way that you can't come up with new ones anymore. So before we start looking at practical ways to vet ideas, let's make sure we're on the same page when it comes to the principles of vetting. We'll go over three principles that have really helped me in the idea-vetting process: principles that have helped me focus on the best ideas without hampering my ability to come up with new ideas. They are the Jelly Bean Principle, the Innocence Principle, and the Craftsman Principle.

The Jelly Bean Principle

Though my wife and I don't eat a lot of sweets (we're more into savory foods like cheese, meat, cheese, and potatoes), we do keep a container of jelly beans on the counter. It's not your usual jelly bean container, though. Instead of a bowl that you can sift through, we put them in a small bottle-like holder with an opening that's only big enough for one or two beans to slip out at a time.

Here's the problem: both Laura and I really love about five of those jelly bean flavors, and there are about 50 flavors in the jugs we buy at Costco. (I know we could just buy our favorite flavors, but I guess we just like the idea of getting a year's worth of jelly beans for 11 bucks.) That means every time we tip our jelly bean holder over to get a bean, we're only about 10% likely to get one we really like. So, I'll often just shake around 10 beans out of the container into my hand and pick out the flavor I want.

Our minds are kind of like that jelly bean jar. It's easier to find the best ideas by shaking out a bunch of them and then picking through them until we find the best.

Why is this important? This is an important principle to keep in mind when you're vetting blog posts, because in many ways, this is just the second half of getting ideas. Sometimes you will need to come up with 10 ideas just to find one that's right for your blog. And that's OK, because just like not every jelly bean that comes out of the container is one that I want, not every idea that comes to mind needs to be a winner.

If you keep this in mind, the vetting process won't hurt your idea generation process, either. In fact, it might motivate you to churn out even more ideas to weed through!

The Innocence Principle

This is an important one for any blogger, but it's especially key for those of you who manage a blog that other writers contribute to.

You know the legal saying, "innocent until proven guilty?" That's the approach you should take to vetting ideas. Think of vetting ideas as a filtering process. I'm going to walk you through five filters that you'll be applying to every idea, and what you'll find is that a lot of really interesting ideas aren't going to make it through all five.

This means you'll be tempted to think of those ideas that don't make it as "bad," and the vetting process is set up to keep bad ideas out of your blog. However, that's not an entirely accurate perspective. It's good to come up with ideas, because that's where the good ideas come from. (In fact, if you keep the Jelly Bean principle in mind, coming up with bad ideas may be essential to coming up with good ideas.)

So in the blogging sense, all ideas begin as "good" ideas. All ideas are great until proven otherwise, they're "innocent until proven guilty." This means that in the vetting process, all ideas should be considered good ideas until proven otherwise. It's easier to weed out the ideas that aren't a good fit for your blog than it is to assume all ideas are unworthy until proven otherwise.

The Craftsman Principle

Have you ever had someone shoot down one of your ideas? I have (actually, it's happened to me a lot). It doesn't feel good. In fact, even when it's done tactfully, it hurts. That means the vetting process can be painful. This is important for us to keep in mind, because:

• If you're managing a team of writers, you're going to need to know how to vet ideas without crushing your writers' creativity.

• If you are a writer, you need a method for coming up with ideas that vet well.

I assume that you've been reminded that you and your ideas are separate. You know that someone can reject your idea without necessarily rejecting you. You know this. But that doesn't necessarily make the idea-vetting process easier. Why not?

I think it's because we like to identify with our work. We love coming up with great ideas, and getting told that they're great ideas. I don't believe that identifying with our work is a bad thing, either. However, when we do so this early in the blogging game (at the idea level), we make it difficult to vet our ideas—which makes it really tough to focus on the posts that will be best for our blogs.

So if we're going to identify with our work, and if we can't afford to get in our own way, **we need to change the work we identify with**. Instead of identifying with the ideas themselves, we need to identify with the finished piece. I've found it best to leave my ideas totally open to improvement, input, and maybe rejection, because it allows me to only work on the best.

I call this the Craftsman Principle, because a master craftsman focuses on making the very best products: the best buildings, the best art, the best [whatever he makes]. Does that mean he has the best ideas? Maybe. But his identity is wrapped up in the finished product, not the product concept sketches.

When we vet blog post ideas, we (editors and writers) need to assess them with the end goal in mind: creating a post that helps and resonates with our audience. The best bloggers don't need to have the best ideas, but they do need to publish the best posts.

Moving on

These principles should give you a good idea of what I mean when I talk about vetting ideas. When you have these three principles in mind, the next portion of this chapter will come a lot easier, because:

• You won't expect 100% of your ideas to be winners, because you need to generate several non-winning ideas in order to get a winner (the Jelly Bean Principle).

• You'll be comfortable with subjecting your ideas to the vetting filters, because all ideas are good until proven otherwise (the Innocence Principle).

• You'll be OK with rejecting your own ideas—or having your ideas rejected—because you identify more with the end result than the beginning idea (the Craftsman Principle).

Now that we've prepped ourselves for the gauntlet, lets' take a look at what those five vetting filters are, shall we?

8

THE FIVE FILTERS

We know that not all blog post ideas are going to make it onto our blog. But how are we supposed to know what makes a good blog post and what doesn't? I've put together a list of five big filters to use when you're vetting blog posts. I suggest running every blog post idea through this series of five yes/no filters—if at any point the answer is a hard "no," set it aside and don't move forward with it. If the answer is a "maybe," either spend some research time to see if you can move the answer to a hard "yes" or "no," or set the post idea aside and circle back to it at a later time.

One other note: I recommend running through these filters in the order that I've written them—I've arranged them in this order to streamline the process, so you don't have to do a great deal of research on every idea just to chuck it at the next filter.

Here we go!

1. Is the idea in alignment with your guardrails?

This is the first question you should ask. Even if you have a fabulous, potentially viral blog post idea, it needs to line up with the guardrails you've set for your blog. Otherwise, you'll be spinning your wheels.

For example, let's say you're a tech startup in South Dakota, and your primary audience is 40-something working mothers who want to manage their errands more easily. You *could* post a video entitled, "If motherhood were a first-person shooter video game," and it would probably be hilarious. In fact, it might even be a viral hit. But a video like that probably isn't going to pull in anyone who's actually interested in your courses.

In short, you could be famous, but unless you're famous among the people you want to attract, it won't do you much good.

So, how do you know if your post is in alignment? Check your guardrails (which we covered two chapters ago). Is the post idea something that appeals to your audience? Will it fit within the scope of subject matter your blog is meant to cover? And does it align with your brand's stance on the subject matter?

This is a good place to determine whether a post idea should live on your blog or as a guest post on someone else's blog. Sometimes an idea will come up that not only appeals to your own audience, but to a larger audience as well. When this happens, think of blogs that your audience reads that have a larger readership than your own blog—it may be that you've come up with an idea that you should pursue, but shouldn't necessarily house on your blog.

For example, let's imagine once again that you're that tech startup in South Dakota. You have an idea for a blog post entitled, "30 social media apps moms should know about." That's going to appeal to a lot of people! This is a blog post that your potential customers would love to know about, but potential customers of larger organizations would profit from it as well. If you had an idea like this, I would recommend pitching it to a blog like Buffer's or LifeHacker's. Ideas like these may be a little bit outside your guardrails, but they can still move forward in the vetting process.

2. Is this a unique contribution?

Once you've determined that a blog post idea fits within your blogging guardrails, it's time to see if the idea is a unique contribution to the online discussion.

To me, this is one of the most important things to hold in mind throughout the entire blogging process. The Internet is filled, no, littered with blog posts—and they're not all unique. I'm not just talking about plagiarism, either (though that's a huge issue in the blogosphere). Lots of these posts will have the same kind of content in them, without giving anything new, meaningful, or useful to the reader.

When you write a blog post, you want to make sure you're not just adding to the noise. You want to write something that will be useful to the audience you're trying to attract—so useful that it makes them want to know more and more about you.

You need to contribute something unique to the online conversation.

I like to think of the blogosphere as a great big dinner party with thousands of little circles of people talking about what they're interested in. Each circle represents the online conversation surrounding a certain topic, and each person speaking in these conversations is a blog.

At the ideal blog dinner party, each person in the circle is sharing what they know, asking questions about what they don't know, getting to know the people with the answers, and listening for helpful and interesting information. However, we've all been to dinner parties. We know that not everyone knows what they're talking about—in fact, in any circle there's going to be that one guy who just repeats what the others are saying without saying anything new (or he restates their insight in his own words).

You don't want to be that guy. You want to be one of the people in that circle who knows what they're talking about, and talks about it in such a way that benefits the people listening. That's why each blog post idea needs to be vetted against the online conversation that's already happening around that topic.

But obviously there's more to it than just deciding to be a conversation contributor. In order to contribute to the conversation, you need to know two things:

1. What has already been said

2. What has been left out

Let's get a brief, practical overview of how to assess the online conversation using two tools: Google and Buzzsumo.

Using Google to assess the conversation

Once you know a blog post idea fits your guardrails, the first thing you should do is Google that idea. This will help you see which pages people are already reading on the idea.

For our example, let's say you have an idea for a blog post about the most beautiful corporate campus in each state. You're going to make a list of 50 company campuses. It sounds like a great idea—especially if you have the most beautiful place in your state!

But before you start writing that brilliant-sounding post, you want see what's already out there.

To do this, Google "most beautiful workplaces by state." Then open all the results on the first page. You're now looking at a spread of what people looking for gorgeous workspaces find when they search the Web. Now, read through each of these results and ask yourself three questions:

- "What's helpful?"
- "What's not helpful?
- "Could I do better?"

This very simple activity gives you a huge advantage when it comes to vetting your blog post ideas. If the Internet is already chock-full of articles on this idea, and you don't think you can do any better than any of the top 10 results, then you know not to waste your time on this piece. But that's rarely going to happen. More often than not, you'll get plenty of ideas for how to refine your blog post idea in light of what's already been written. You'll discover influencers in your space. You'll see how far the online conversation has progressed already. And you'll identify information gaps that you can fill.

But Google isn't the end-all tool for assessing the online conversation. We also need to get an idea of what's trending on social media. For that, I recommend Buzzsumo.

Using Buzzsumo to assess the conversation

Buzzsumo is one of my favorite marketing tools, hands-down. Without getting too technical, it's a tool that lets you find the most popular Web pages:

- on a given topic
- by a given author

- on a given website

It's rather incredible. And you can use some of its features for free (though I highly, highly recommend the paid version).

That sounds cool, but you might be wondering, "Why do I need another tool? Didn't Google pretty much cover this?" The answer is, "Not really," and here's why.

There's more to blogging than just writing. You also need a post that you (and your readers!) can promote. If you've planned your blog well, a great deal of your traffic is going to come from your readers sharing it on social media—which means you need to see what those readers are sharing on social media now. If you can see what people are sharing, you can better understand whether or not this post idea is going to contribute to the online conversation.

I don't think this is the place to give a software tutorial, but I have listed two ways to use Buzzsumo to assess the online conversation.

1. See what works for the influencers. If you know which experts or celebrities your audience follows, you can look them up in Buzzsumo to see what their most popular articles are. This will give you some insight on what people are most excited or frustrated about in the online community.

2. See what works for your competitors. Plug their website URL into the Buzzsumo bar and see which of their pages and blog posts are getting the most traction.

Are you contributing?

If you've looked at the content that has already been published and you're confident that you're not just adding to the noise, terrific! That blog post idea has made it through two of the five filters. Now it's time to face the third one: demand.

3. Is there sufficient demand for this?

We've been dealing with subjectives up until this point. Now it's time to drill into something a little bit more concrete: demand.

This is one of the bits of blogging that often goes overlooked, usually because if something sounds like a great idea, most bloggers will just go for it. However, it helps to make sure there's some degree of demand for the information you're thinking about making available. It would be a shame to spend 10 hours crafting an excellent infographic and a 2,000-word blog post only to launch it to crickets. That's why it's helpful to assess the demand for a blog post in the vetting stages.

I like to think about demand as being loosely divided into two categories: current demand and potential demand.

A content idea has current demand if people are regularly searching for it on Google, shopping for it on Amazon, liking and sharing it on social media, or even just asking you to create some content around it. A content idea has potential demand when there's a possibility that people will want it after it's created. Sometimes future events awaken demand for certain information. Sometimes the content awakens demand itself by presenting information your audience didn't know they wanted.

The sweet spot is to write blog posts with plenty of current and potential demand. Here's how I assess a whether or not a blog post has either.

Assessing current demand

The first thing to do when you're assessing current demand for a blog post idea is to find out if anyone's already looking for that information online. To do this, we'll need to use Google AdWords' Keyword Planner. The Keyword Planner is a tool that allows you to see how many times a month people will Google a certain search term. You're going to use this tool to see how in-demand your blog post idea is.

Heads-up: it's about to get a little technical. You've noticed that I've tried to keep this guide both conceptual and practical so you don't get bogged down (or bored!) with the details. But this step is so crucial that I want to make sure you have a very, very clear idea of how to assess the current demand of a post. Therefore, I'm going to give you a brief tutorial on Google's Keyword Planner.

You can access this tool by going to Adwords.Google.com/keywordplanner. (It's also the first result when you Google "keyword planner.") You can create a free AdWords account, log in, and then start having fun with Google's data.

Now, let's say you wanted to write a blog post on the best college campuses in the United States. You first want to see what people are searching for on that topic. So, start by clicking on "Search for new keyword and ad group ideas."

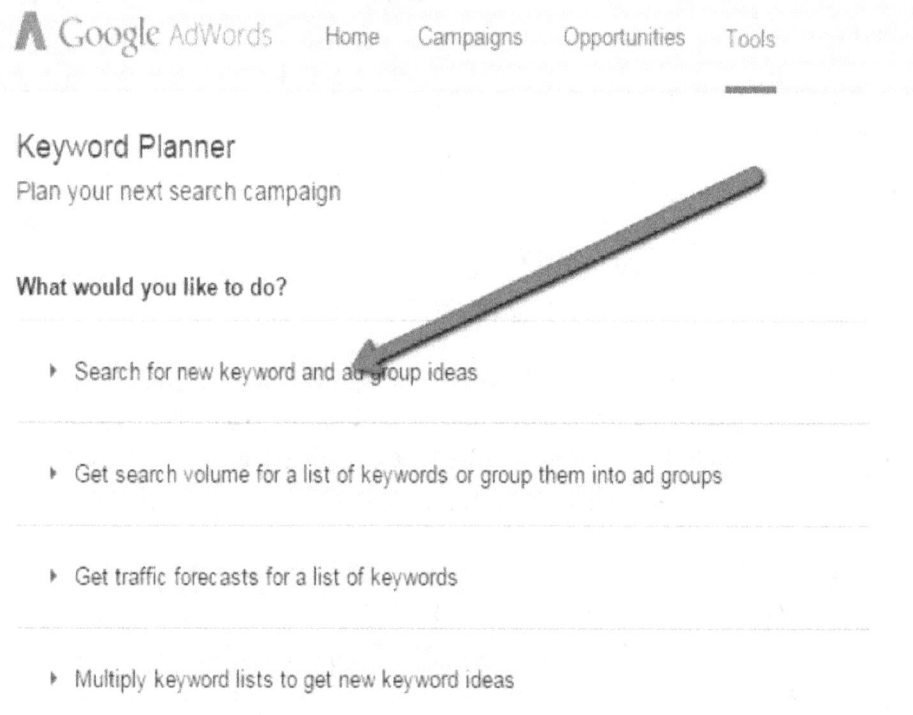

This tells the Keyword Planner that you're not necessarily looking for how many times one specific keyword is searched—you want to get data on how many times similar searches are made, too. When you click this, you will be prompted to plug in your topic. For this example, we'll enter "best corporate campus," and we'll filter it down to searches within the United States.

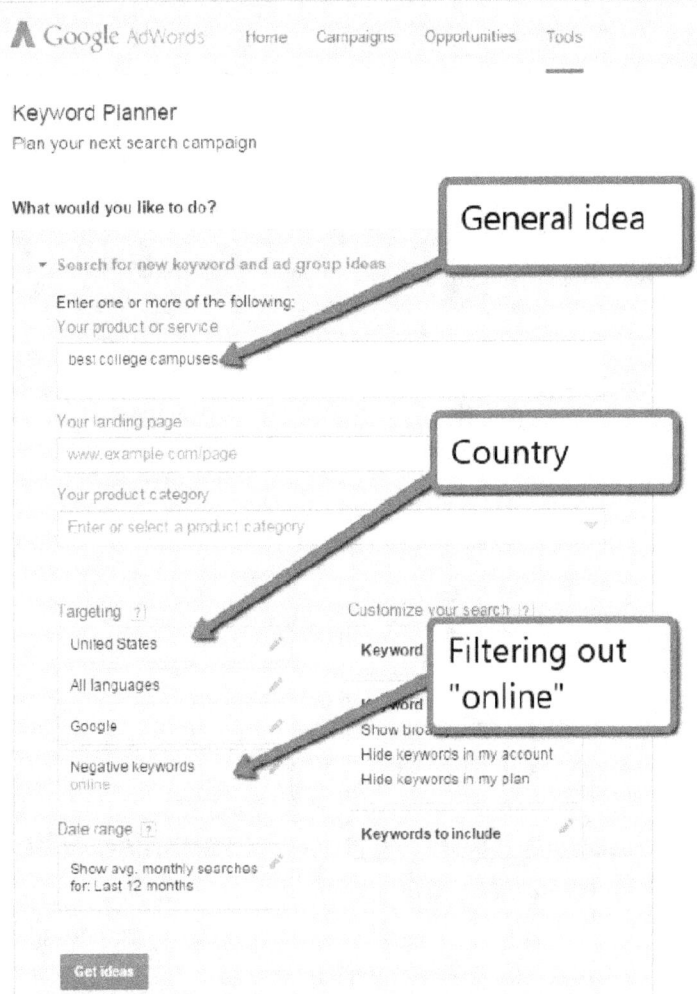

We'll hit "Get ideas," and voila! We get a bunch of related search terms grouped by association. But of course, this is all computerized output—we need something a little more intelligent. So we don't look at the graph up top. Instead, we look at the "Ad group" ideas that actually line up with the blog post idea we have in mind.

We can see that of all the results, at least three groups are close to our blog post idea. And those groups have a total of about 9,200 searches per month.

That's a good amount of searches—this is a post idea that I would say has decent current demand.

This is quantifiable, but AdWords isn't everything. There isn't always a lot of search traffic for things in demand. Sometimes the target audience is too niche for impressive search volume like this—and so I wouldn't use Google as the end-all test. It's just a good place to start. There are other ways to see if your blog post idea is in demand:

• If you hear more than one person ask a question (and neither knows that the other person asked it), there's at least some current demand for the answer.

• You can email the people on your email list to see if your blog idea is something they would like to see an article on. Normally it's good to give them an either/or scenario: you present them with two blog post ideas and see which one they're more drawn to.

- Remember Buzzsumo? You can look up articles on your idea and see if any related articles have significant shares on social media.

These are a few ways to know if anyone is interested in reading content related to your blog post idea. Now let's look at ways to assess whether or not your idea has potential demand.

Assessing potential demand

This one is a little tougher. Current demand is a great thing to have in mind: you want to know what people are looking for today. But you also what to have an idea of what people will be looking for tomorrow, too.

There are a few ways to assess potential demand, but before we get into them, I want to distinguish two kinds of potential demand to have in mind when it comes to writing blog posts.

1. External potential demand is demand for an idea that arises from outside your organization. This could be sparked by current events, new movies, or some random viral video. This is tough to plan for, because you don't have many ways (outside of corporate espionage!) to divine what's coming down the pipeline outside your company. However, if you monitor the blogs and websites of competitors and influencers in your audience's space, you will stand a better chance of seeing where the conversation is going.

One tool that can help immensely in doing research on external potential demand is Google Trends. This tool lets you view Google search data over time to see when searches typically peak. You can also see if the general interest in your idea is trending upward or downward. For example, you can see in which month people most often search for "Bachelors of Business Administration," and plan to launch your blog post about the best BBAs in the nation accordingly.

2. Internal potential demand is generated by what you as a blogger or organization do and say. This is not as nebulous as external potential demand, because you (should) know what you're up to! However, results are still the big unknown factor. You might be launching a brand new product, or introducing a new executive, or getting awesome new ping-pong tables. A fraction of your existing audience would be very interested in learning more, but probably not everyone.

Measuring internal potential demand can be tricky, but I recommend starting with your existing internal statistics. Look at the emails you've sent to your leads in the last six months. What has been the average open rate? What percentage of recipients click through your emails? How many visitors does your blog get on a given day? When you know how your audience engages with you online, you can have a loose idea of how they will engage with future content you produce.

Moving on

So, you've looked at the current and potential demand your blog post idea has. Is it sufficient? Are there enough people in your audience looking for this content? If so, move that idea on to the next filter!

---

4. Does the post idea have sufficient longevity?

If your post idea has made it this far, it's more than halfway there! This is actually one of the kinder filters I use for vetting blog posts. It's the longevity filter, and it's a simple assessment of how long the post will be relevant.

When I put it that way, it might sound like there is a certain amount of time a post should be relevant before you pass it on to the next (and final) filter. But that's not really the case. There's no magical longevity number, no target relevance period, no ideal timeline when it comes to how timely a post may be. The question is simply, "Is this post going to last long enough to pay off?"

Some posts take the authors about 15 minutes to write and go viral, paying off for years! (My friend Teryn O'Brien wrote a terrific example—this quick post has racked up more than two million views.) Other blog posts will take ten hours to create, not go viral, but sustain traffic anyway. Case in point: here's my best-performing post.

But for the purposes of this chapter, let's focus on two major types of longevity you need to have in mind when vetting a blog post: **content longevity** and **audience longevity**. The first deals with how long the post itself will be relevant. The second has more to do with how long the audience you attract will stick around.

Content longevity

Content longevity is the more straightforward of the two concepts, so let's discuss this first. Content longevity is the measure of time a given piece of content will be relevant to your audience. That might be a very brief span of time, or it could be the kind of information that just never gets old.

We encounter blog posts with very low content longevity all the time. The most common example is the category of news blogs. Many news networks, newspapers, and local TV stations post articles on their websites about current events—sometimes updating the stories multiple times a day as new information is released. These posts are like mayflies: alive today and dead tomorrow, buried under the next news story.

Then you have the opposite extreme: posts with very, very high content longevity. In the marketing world, we call these kinds of posts **evergreen**. You can guess why: these posts don't lose relevance over time, so they're always in season. These posts keep their long-tail appeal because their content is both interesting and not subject to change. For example, a blog post analyzing the imperative verbs in the Bill of Rights will be interesting to law students for a long time, and the Bill of Rights isn't going to change anytime soon, so that post won't expire.

Granted, a good amount of your blog posts will be somewhere in between. You don't always need to shoot for evergreen blog posts, but since you probably don't have time to churn out brand-new, timely blog posts day in and day out, I suggest erring on the side of more content longevity.

But there's more to the longevity story than how long the content will be relevant. We also need to know about the crowd your content will attract—whether your content is evergreen or not.

How do you measure content longevity? There are a few scientific ways to measure content longevity, as well as a few intuitive ones.

Use Google Trends. This free tool visualizes the aggregate Google searches since 2004, and lets you see how specific search terms rise and fall over time. For example, if you wanted to know whether or not a blog post about college scholarships had any content longevity, you could plug the search term, "college scholarships" into Google Trends. Here's what you'd see:

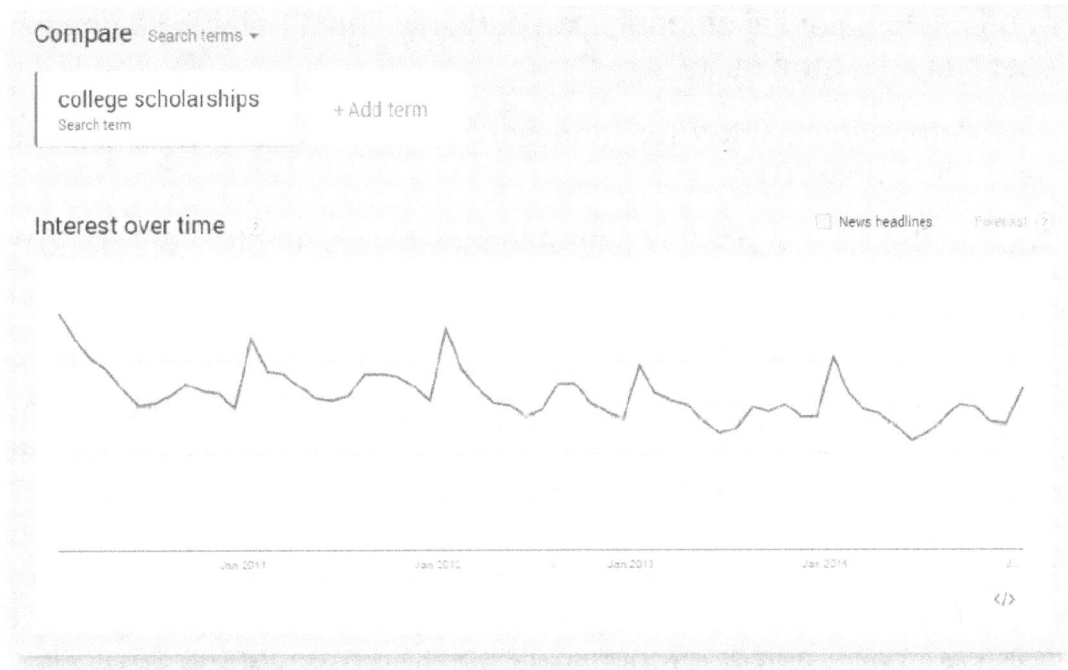

Since 2010, the term has seen a spike at the beginning of each year (when kids and their parents start looking for ways to save on tuition), and the search volume isn't on a drastic downward trajectory. From a search standpoint, the idea has a good deal of content longevity.

Check for long-term utility. It's not good enough to simply write a post on college scholarships—or any search term with long-tail search volume, for that matter. You also need to consider whether or not the idea you have in mind will be useful in the long run. Let's keep running with the example of a college scholarship blog post to illustrate. We've seen that "college scholarships" has long-term appeal, but what about these specific post ideas related to that search term?

• "20 college scholarships in New Hampshire for female students"—this list of scholarships probably isn't going to change very rapidly, and female potential students can certainly find it helpful. I'd say this post has long-term utility.

- "College scholarships for homeschoolers in 2016"—well, this will have utility until 2017.

You get the idea: a post's content longevity is a function of how long that post will be able to help your audience.

Can it be authoritative? This is the most subjective of the content longevity questions. If you've made it this far through the vetting process, you already know you're making a unique contribution to the online conversation. Now it's time to ask the soul-searching question: can this post be authoritative on the subject matter? Will it be well-researched enough to be taken seriously by the readers? Will it by well-written enough to be compelling to the readers? Will it be comprehensive enough for readers to say, "Wow. I've hit the jackpot with this. Everything's here!"

(We'll get into this later, but most of these posts are more than 2,000 words long, they link out to a lot of other authoritative sources, and they're full of practical, actionable content.)

You might be thinking, "That sounds like a lot of work. Does my post need to be authoritative?" No, not every post you write needs to be authoritative. But an authoritative post is naturally going to have more content longevity built into it. That's because authoritative posts stand above the rest of the content other blogs are churning out. Authoritative posts are the ones other bloggers like to link to. Authoritative posts are the ones that are cited as sources in other authoritative posts, news stories, or even Wikipedia articles.

There's a lot of benefit to writing the authoritative blog post on a subject, especially in terms of content longevity.

Audience longevity

When we talk about audience longevity in terms of blog posts, we're referring to how long the audience a piece of content attracts will stick around. An evergreen blog post will pull in new readers long-term, but if it has low audience longevity, then that steady stream of readers won't be following you for very long. But if a post has high audience longevity, it will win the people who read it over to you, and they will keep coming back to your blog for more.

By the way, if the blog post idea you're considering is going to be a guest post on someone else's blog, audience longevity is even more important than content longevity. You're putting your content on another property in hopes that some of your host's audience will take interest in you. Therefore, you want to make sure it will attract as many loyal people to you as possible.

How do you tell if a post has audience longevity? It's a lot simpler than determining whether or not it has content longevity. If you've set up your audience guardrails (please, please tell me it's true!), you already know whom you're trying to bring to your blog. Now it's just a question of whether or not this post idea will bring in that audience.

There are a few questions you can ask to help you determine whether a post idea has audience longevity:

- What specific problem does this post help my audience solve?

- Is this enough to keep a new visitor coming back to me for more?

If it solves a specific problem that your target audience has in a way that makes them want to hear more from you, then you probably have a blog post idea with some audience longevity.

You can probably see why I've split content and audience longevities apart. You could write a blog post with very, very low content longevity that pulls in a great deal of new readers who want to keep coming back to you for more excellent content. And as long as you have a means of keeping them coming back for more (hint: email newsletter signups!), even a post that's only good for 24 hours can be a huge win for your blog if it attracts the kind of audience that will stick around for a while.

Moving on

In case I haven't made it clear already, there's no magic longevity score you need to hit with every blog post. The real question is, are you satisfied with both the content and audience longevity the post idea has? If so, move on to the final filter! If not, it's time to put this idea on ice—it just doesn't have the staying power that you need from your blog posts.

Is it worth the cost?

This one's pretty straightforward. Before greenlighting any blog post idea for being outlined and thrown into the hopper to be written, you need to square away whether or not it will be worth the cost to produce.

That cost is threefold. When you're considering the cost of a blog post, you should consider three aspects of the cost:

1. Material cost

This involves the money and resources you need to give up in order to make the content work. This includes the costs that go into production, and those costs vary greatly from idea to idea. For example, you may need to hire a designer to create an infographic. You may need to hire a photographer to cover an event. In some cases, you may need to drive or fly somewhere to interview someone in person. Or you may just need to drop a few dollars for a stock photo.

But the material cost of a blog idea isn't restricted to the production of a post. It also involves any promotional resources you'll use for the post. How much money will you spend promoting it on Facebook, Twitter, and Google? (It's OK if the answer is "none," this is just something you need to consider up front.)

Material cost is important, especially if you're on a tight budget. But the next kind of cost is even more important to consider.

2. Opportunity cost

This is one of the harsh realities of blogging: every idea you spend time on is taking time from something else. It could be taking time from promoting your existing material. It could be taking time from writing a more useful post. It could be taking time from answering an important email or following up with a hot lead.

This is one reason it's helpful to separate the vetting process from the idea generation process. If you vet ideas one-by-one as they come to you, you won't be able to assess them in the context of other ideas you have. But by generating plenty of ideas and then vetting them as a group later, you can focus on the ones that clearly deserve your attention more than others.

When you're vetting ideas by opportunity cost, ask yourself these questions:

• How much time will this take to produce?

• How much time will this take to promote?

• Where is that time going to come from? Where will I make room for it?

- Is there anything I could be doing that would be a better use of my time instead?

- What about the material costs of this post—could those be better spent elsewhere?

- If I move forward, what results should I expect?

When you've looked at the material and opportunity costs, it's time to assess the idea's overall cost.

Go, Woah, No, or So?

I find it helpful to think in terms of a grid when it comes to vetting the cost of a blog idea. On one axis is value, and on the other is bargain.

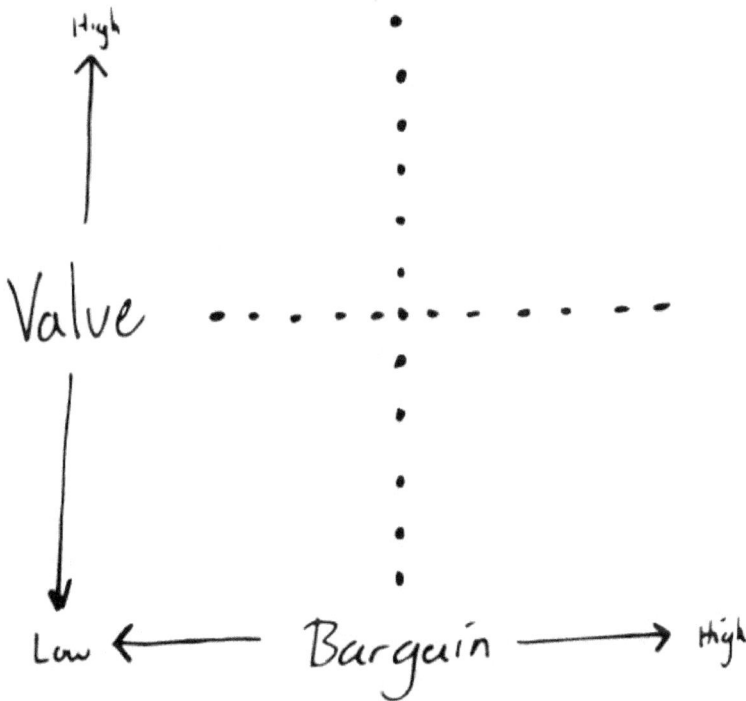

In this case, I think of value as the return I'll make off a certain idea. There are many ways to measure value. A valuable post could acquire 500 new customers or clients. A valuable post could get your brand featured by a prominent publication in your industry. A valuable post could make your customers feel like they're heard and appreciated.

I think we all understand what bargain means! If something doesn't cost you a lot in terms of time, money, or other resources, that's a bargain.

If you divvy that grid down the middle both ways, you get four quadrants—or, as I like to think of them, Go, Woah, No, and So?

Here's what those quadrants represent:

Go (high value, great bargain). This is the top-right quadrant. Sometimes you'll get an idea that has potential to drive a lot of traffic, generate a lot of leads, and/or win a lot of contracts—and it won't cost you much. Those are the "Go" posts: they're no-brainers. Run with them!

Whoa (high value, not a great bargain). Sometimes you'll have golden ideas for posts—but they come at a price. They may require half a week of research. They may require a lot of design work. Or they might need buy-in from so many stakeholders that the approval process is the main expense.

As you can imagine, a lot of awesome ideas fall into this category. That doesn't mean you shouldn't execute on them, but it helps to put on the brakes and see if you can trim that idea down to size. That's where the "Whoa" comes from. When you have an idea like this, stop to consider ways you might be able to execute on it at a better bargain. Does it really need all the bells and whistles?

It may still be worth your while to write a "Whoa" post. Great content isn't necessarily cheap. It's just good to make sure you're knocking out the quick-win "Go" ideas first.

No (low value, not a great bargain). If you've been vetting your ideas well thus far, you shouldn't have too many falling into this category. But every once in a while, you'll look at an idea you had earlier and think, "Wait a second. This idea will take up a lot of my time without really gaining me all that much." If it's in the "No" quadrant, throw it out.

So? (low value, great bargain). This is the most frustrating category. Sometimes you'll get ideas (and often you'll be given ideas by others) that can be quickly or inexpensively done, but just can't yield a good return. That's why I call this quadrant "So?"—because if you can't answer the question, "So what do we get out of this?" you probably shouldn't move forward with the blog post.

That doesn't mean all "So?" blog posts are hopeless and useless. In fact, you might be able to refine a "So?" idea into a "Go" idea if you focus on ways to make the post more valuable. That might look like brainstorming to find a killer lead-generating offer. It might look like expanding the post so that it has a chance of ranking on search engines.

Now that you've looked at the blog's costs, it's time to ask the big question: **Is it worth it?**

If not, it's time to move on to the next idea in your content well.

But if it is worth it, then congratulations! Your post is green-lighted and ready for the next stage: strategizing the content.

9

WHY WE STRATEGIZE BLOG POSTS

We've looked at how to fill your content well with blog post ideas, and how to decide which ideas become blog posts and which ones don't. This is when most bloggers would jump right into the writing process. (Well, it's what I used to do, at least.) By this time, you're revved up about a blog idea that has passed your vetting test with flying colors. You want to start bringing your idea to life. I understand the feeling, but in this chapter, I'm going to walk you through one last important phase to go through before you start writing. That's the phase of strategizing your blog post.

You've probably heard the word "strategy" in many contexts. Some people use it to refer to plans that span five years or more. Some people use it as another word for "vision," or "big picture." Since we've all been exposed to different people using the term in different ways, let's take a moment to make sure we're on the same page when we're talking about strategizing a blog post.

It's pretty simple: **A blog post strategy is your plan for how a blog post will be produced, promoted, and evaluated.**

Why we strategize blog posts

We're going to look at how to lay out such a plan for every blog post you write. But first, there's a big issue we need to get out of the way when it comes to blog post strategy. It's a perspective issue that can make the difference between great strategies, terrible strategies, and no strategies at all.

The issue? The desire for productivity.

We don't normally think of the desire for productivity as a problem. (And we won't at the end of this section, either.) But the ways we want to be productive, or the things that make us feel productive can get in the way of us creating outstanding blog posts.

Specifically, our desire to be productive can make the strategy phase of blogging feel like a waste of time. This was something I struggled with for a while when I started blogging. I was on the clock. I needed to spend my time working, and in my mind, taking the time to map out blog posts was not work. There were two reasons I thought that strategy was a poor use of work time:

1. Strategy felt like too much fun.

2. I was thinking of productivity in terms of pieces written, not in terms of the results they brought in.

Maybe you deal with this, too. You'd rather feel like you're working than spend time planning work out. It may seem like the strategy phase is a waste of time you could spend writing (or working on something else).

Or, perhaps you'd rather feel more "in the moment" when you're writing: you want to discover where your blog post is going as you're writing it. It may seem like the strategy phase is a creative block: something that will rob you of the artistic process of writing compelling, beautiful prose.

But here's the deal: writing blog posts without strategizing them will not scale.

Strategy doesn't merely help us write better content. It helps us build a system that allows us to write more of it. Even if you write fantastic, non-strategized, "organic" blog posts, you will get an increase in demand for those posts. Then what? You'll either pass up on the opportunity (not advised), lower the quality of your posts to increase the quantity (also not advised), or create a system that empowers you to write more terrific posts. That's where the strategy comes in.

Let's spend a little bit of time looking at the ways a blog post strategy will help us, and then jump into some practical ways to strategize blog posts.

1. Strategy helps us write

When you sit down to write, you should be able to sit down and write.

For years, when I wanted to write a blog post, I would sit down with an idea in mind, and unfold that idea paragraph by paragraph. Unfortunately, those paragraphs didn't come quickly. I had to research the ideas I had. I had to rewrite and rearrange the sentences so that one paragraph wouldn't seem out of place. I was constantly distracting myself by combining the planning, writing, and editing processes of my blog post into one session—and it took forever to write anything!

Strategizing a blog post will help. In fact, strategizing posts is how a great deal of prolific, authoritative voices in the blogging world produce the volume of content they make. It's not getting more ideas or improving typing speed. And it's certainly not finding more time to write (there's never more time). Blogger and entrepreneur Danny Iny wrote in an email once:

> The reason most people struggle with writing is that there are actually two "phases" to the writing process (not counting editing), and they try to do them both at the same time:
>
> 1. Figuring out which ideas you want to share (in which order).
>
> 2. Choosing the words to communicate the ideas.
>
> In other words, there's the PLANNING of what you'll write, and there's the actual WRITING of the content.
>
> Most people try to do them at the same time, and that's really tough; it means your writing times will be a LOT slower.
>
> If you plan out your content in advance, though, you can speed up a lot; I can usually do 1,200-1,700 really good words in an hour if I've got a good outline to work from.
>
> That's the key: detailed, detailed outlines.

We'll get into how to create those detailed outlines later in this chapter. But for now, it's important to know that even if nobody ever sees how your blog post strategy influences your writing (which we'll get to next), there's still a huge advantage that you get from the process. A strategy helps you produce more content, faster.

Why? Because when you create a strategy for your blog post, you're working entirely with your line of thought. You're not hung up on the need to flesh that line of thought out for your reader—you're just focusing on organizing your ideas in a way that makes sense. Once you've laid out that pathway, it's easier to follow.

In other words, think of your mind as a locomotive, not an all-terrain vehicle.

You can take your ATV anywhere: road or no road. You can ride along rough trails or blaze your own. It's easy to turn around if you feel like you've gone the wrong way, and it's easy to change course if you really want to see what's beyond that next hill. ATVs are built for exploring.

A locomotive, though? You don't want to explore in those. They need tracks laid down ahead of time, with a clear destination and plenty of fuel. That's because trains aren't for joy rides. Trains are for getting stuff done: delivering thousands of tons of cargo to the right destination on time.

Now, when it comes to writing authoritative, relevant content, you want to treat your mind like a locomotive. Your mind is a powerful content-creating machine, and you will make it a lot easier for it to deliver if you lay out the tracks first!

A good strategy helps us write blog posts. We'll get into how to create a blog outline toward the end of this chapter; first we need to understand a few more ways strategy helps.

2. Strategy helps us plan for readers

A good blog post will be easy for your readers to consume, and your blog post strategy helps you make sure that's the kind of post you're writing. When you strategize first, you come up with the angle the post will take. You flesh out that unique contribution this post makes to the online conversation, and you plan your post in such a way that your readers understand why this post isn't like the others. A good strategy will answer these questions before you ever start writing the post:

- Why would your audience read this post?

- What will your audience do in response, and why?

- What specific questions does this post answer?

- What specific challenges does this post help your audience overcome?

- Why would your audience trust or share this post?

Strategy helps you form your post in a way that makes sense to the most important people: your readers. Later in this chapter, we will take a closer look at how to plan your blog post in such a way that people will want to read it.

3. Strategy helps us plan for robots

People aren't the only ones who read your blog. Search engines like Google are also looking at your content, but for a very different reason. These search engines look at what you've written, where you've written it, what you link to, and where your traffic is coming from. They index your blog posts so that later on, they might be able to recommend those posts to people searching online for what you've written.

Of course, the robots notice some things humans don't care about. They look at the technical aspects of your blog: the main words in your headline, the density of those words in your article, the alt text of your images, etc. A good blog post strategy not only helps you plan a post that will be well-read by the people in your audience; it also helps you plan a post that Google readily suggests to your audience!

4. Strategy helps us plan for promotion

This is crucial. Most bloggers will write a post and hope it takes off on its own. A small percentage of bloggers write a post and only afterwards try to come up with ways to promote it. But you can gain the advantage: you can plan your promotion before and during the writing process—this way, when you publish it, you already know exactly how you're going to drive traffic to it.

"Promotion? What about editorial integrity?"

This question is more specific to some industries than others, so if that never crossed your mind, just skip to the "How to plan for people" segment below. But if you do have a publications background, I understand why planning for promotion might sound a little weird.

"Promotion" doesn't necessarily mean beating your corporate chest within your own content (though there are times when that's very appropriate). You won't use each blog post to exclusively push your own product—in fact, some of your posts may be entirely audience-serving content that doesn't mention you at all. However, every single post you write should be promoted in some way, even if it's just asking your employees and co-workers to tell their friends about it.

That's because even if you've written a fantastic blog post, it will take a long time to bring in traffic on its own. You will need to give it a little "push," if you will: enough traffic for it to begin getting shared and linked to from other sites.

So when I talk about planning for promotion, I'm referring to planning your blog post in such a way that you will know how to start driving traffic to it. Trust me—you do not want to pour a lot of hard work into a blog post only to hit "Publish" and then … crickets. It's better to structure your post in such a way that you know exactly how to launch it with a bang!

Moving on

I assume we're all on the same page here as far as why we need to strategize our blog posts. Strategy helps us write. It helps our readers enjoy our content. It helps search engines find and rank our content. And it helps us promote it after we've hit "Publish."

Now, let's get a closer look at practical ways to build a blog post strategy. We're going to examine three things to keep in mind before you outline a blog post: people, robots, and promotion.

10

PLANNING BLOG POSTS PEOPLE WANT TO READ

It doesn't matter how authoritative or comprehensive your blog post is unless people want to read it. So before you outline your post, you want to have a very clear idea of how this blog will appeal to the people in your audience.

In short, you need to ask yourself, "Why would anyone care about this post?" The answer to this question is what we'll call the angle.

And you need a good angle.

That good answer could be anything. People could care about this post because it's the most in-depth piece they've ever read on the topic at hand. They might care because they've never heard your side of the story. They might care just because it's laugh-out-loud hilarious.

Whatever the reason, you should have a good idea of why anyone in your audience would be interested in reading this post before you ever start writing it. There are two main reasons I find this rule helpful:

Firstly, it keeps you focused on the reader. There are many obvious reasons you want to stay focused on your readers when you blog. But the most compelling reason (to me) is that when you're focused on your readers, you don't waste time writing self-serving, navel-gazing, "wouldn't-it-be-cool-if-we-published-this?" material.

If you know why people are going to want to read (and keep reading) your piece, you will keep the post centered on that angle. Think of it as a form of pre-customer service: you know what your reader wants, so you want to focus on giving it to them.

Secondly, it saves you time (and creative energy). Most people (myself included) start blogging with an idea in their mind that goes a little something like this: "What if I wrote an article on the best widgets for potential customers to consider?"

Then we start writing, until halfway through the article we realize, "Oh. Really I should write an article on the top 10 widgets for a certain subset of my audience to pursue." And then we re-work (and sometimes re-re-work) the article to fit the new angle. I've found myself in situations where I've started and stopped on enough for three different articles before I've finally settled on the angle for my piece. It's a waste of time, and it's very frustrating!

So I've adopted a new principle for writing blog posts: I decide on my angle before I even outline a post. Some of my potential angle ideas get thrown into the content well as future blog post ideas. Some angles become subpoints for the article I'm working on. And some are just bad ideas that get thrown out.

So, how are you going to come up with an angle?

As you can imagine, there are many ways you can come up with angles for your blog post ideas. And this is probably a good place to say that coming up with angles is a lot easier for some bloggers than others. Some bloggers are highly creative; they can conjure up interesting ideas naturally. Some bloggers are extremely empathetic; they can infer the problems their readers are struggling with most, and write the post everyone's waiting for. Some bloggers are masterfully persuasive; they can intuit the exact line of reasoning that will get people to take a desired action (and feel really good about it, too).

But these folks are the minority. Most bloggers in the marketing space don't just have angles jumping into their heads all the time at a moment's notice. That's why we need a system for coming up with blog post angles. A system helps us land on a direction for a post, stick with it, and know that we're writing something people will want to read.

You can come up with your own system if you like, but I suppose it would be rather cruel of me to talk about how important angles are and then not show you how I come up with them! So, let's walk through the five questions I answer when I'm developing an angle for my blog post.

1. What specific questions could this article answer?

You have your blog post idea. Now it's time to drill into more specific questions your readers will have on the issue. Your readers will have some questions on their mind before they even know about your article, and they will begin asking new ones as soon as they read the headline. You want to anticipate these questions and prioritize the ones that make the most sense to answer.

At this stage in the game, you will already have an idea of a general question your readers might be asking—otherwise, your idea wouldn't have passed the vetting filter. But now we need to drill into that idea to expose all the subquestions that people will be asking as they read your piece.

Think about your blog post idea and begin asking yourself as many questions about the subject matter as possible. (No questions coming to mind? Start with the tried-and-true five W's and an H: who, what, when, where, why, and how.) I would suggest writing these questions down, as you will generate more than you can remember!

For example, let's say you're a real estate agent in Idaho, and you want to write a post on the advantages and disadvantages of moving to Idaho. Using the 5 W's and an H, you can start peppering that blog post idea with questions the reader might ask:

- What kind of person tends to enjoy living in Idaho?

- What places would I be able to visit in Idaho that I couldn't see anywhere else?

- What's the climate like in Idaho?

- What sort of cultural differences should I expect in Idaho?

That list could be a lot longer, but I think you get the idea.

Write out all the questions that come to mind, and then start filtering them down. There's a good chance that you've raised more questions than a single blog post can answer, and that's not a bad thing. I would suggest writing down the questions most closely-related to your blog post idea, as these are going to inform your angle.

Before we move on to the next step in this process, let's also talk about what to do with all the questions that you will not be addressing in this post. It would be a shame to let these ideas go to waste! Look at all the leftover questions and see if you can group any of them together. Throw those groups back into the content well to vet later. Now, look at the leftover questions that didn't nicely fit with the others. Do any of them sound like blog post ideas? Throw them in the content well, too.

Now that we've come up with questions, let's move on to the next set stage.

2. What's my source of authority?

When we're developing our angle, we're asking, "Why will the audience care about this piece?" Part of answering that question is answering the smaller question, "Why will the audience trust this piece?"

When it comes to the kind of blog posts we're writing, people don't just care about the content. They also care about where it's coming from. You want to create authoritative pieces, and so you need a good idea of where that authority is going to flow from.

Authority can flow from several sources: experts and influencers, research, case studies, etc. And you can tap into that authority in a variety of ways. You could quote an authoritative book. You could link to an authoritative blog post. You could post findings from research you've done (or from research someone else has done). You could even use personal experience as a case study, if that experience is impressive and relevant enough.

Here are a few ways to start planning for your blog post's credibility:

Plan your primary sources ahead of time. Think of books, articles, and other discourses that are already seen as authoritative pieces on the topic at hand. Make a list of these to reference later. You don't need to determine your exact quotes right now, but you will want to have them on hand when you begin writing.

Ask experts for an original quote before you write. Anyone can reference an expert's previously published work, but not every article will have a new bit of content from the experts. Email (or tweet to) an expert on the topic you're writing about, and tell them you would love to get a 1-2 line comment from them for an upcoming article (of course, tell them what it's about). Make it very easy for them to comment, as you don't want to take up too much of their time.

For example, you might tweet the following message to an influencer:

"Hey, @MrsExpertson: what would you say is the biggest pro and biggest con of moving to Idaho? I'd love to quote you in my next post. =)"

Do some research. Think of ways you can give the readers some in-depth information that you yourself have found. You could survey your own customers, or piece together existing (and current!) data from other sources. Don't underestimate how much a little bit of quantitative evidence can do for your content.

Plus, research lends itself very nicely to graphs and charts—things visual learners love to share on social networks.

You may have picked up on a not-so-dirty little secret of the blogosphere: you don't need to be the expert on everything you write about—at least not at the time you begin writing. You just need to write the very best content on the issue at hand, and that usually involves some degree of expert opinion. You can pull that expertise from other sources (and credit them).

But if you're not an expert, and you're still writing the best articles on the subject, you will find that something very special happens: your audience begins to see you as a leader. Even if you're not the one who spent years studying the material. Your readers will appreciate your ability to break down the experts' information in a way that helps them answer questions and overcome obstacles, and they'll keep coming back to you for more.

That may sound a bit sketchy to you. "Wait a minute. So you're telling me that a 20-something kid could be seen as an expert in biochemistry just by quoting and paraphrasing the studies of someone who spent 40 years in that field?"

Yes, that's exactly what could happen. Should that be the case? Maybe not, but there's a good reason it works this way.

In a perfect world, every expert would have N. T. Wright's gift for presenting information in ways that both the elite and the lay majority understand. But that's not the world we live in. In fact, it's almost the opposite: the experts often become so used to speaking and writing for other experts that they lose touch with the hundreds of thousands of people who look up their areas of expertise on Wikipedia every day. The result? Non-experts flooding the lay readers with non-expert content, and experts writing content only other experts can (or will take the time to) consume.

So, how do we set it right? We write, and we write well!

We write the very best blog posts that answer the very best questions with the very best information in the very best way.

And when we do this, when we take it on ourselves to serve our readers with excellent, easy-to-find, easy-to-read, easy-to-use content, we begin to make things right:

• Readers learn more about the topic at hand.

• Experts get more widespread recognition, because they're mentioned in authoritative articles.

- Chintzy articles get less attention.

That's the power of writing credible, authoritative blog posts. And that's why determining your post's source of authority is key to determining your post's angle.

3. **Why will people share this post?**

We've looked at the specific problems your post will solve, and we've looked at why anyone should take it seriously. Now we need to think about another important piece of a blog post's angle: sharability.

Sharability may sound more like something to cover in the promotion section of this chapter, but I'm writing about it here because social media isn't just a channel for promoting your content. Many of your potential customers use social media as their primary source of reading recommendations. Their friends share links to blog posts on Facebook, Twitter, and other networks, and if the headlines and comments look interesting enough, those potential customers read them.

You want to write the kind of articles that get people to read them and share them, so more people read them and share them.

So when you're considering your blog post's angle, ask yourself: Why would anyone share this?

I'll make this question easier by telling you why people share anything: people share things that make them look and feel good. People share cool infographics because they want to be the one to tell their friends about something awesome they found online. People share informative articles because they want to be a source of helpful information to their friends.

Now, think of your article. When someone reads it, is there anything in that article that, if the reader shares it, makes the reader look good? What is that something? It's an important question to answer as you're crafting your angle.

4. **What's the takeaway?**

You've asked yourself about the problems you'll solve, the reasons people should trust you, and the reasons people should share your work. Now comes a different kind of question: what are you giving people? What will they bring from this post? How will this post leave them with more than what they had before?

This is where most blog posts fall flat. Most posts state their case and then come to an end: they don't ask the reader to do anything … except maybe leave a comment. But really, we should be better than that. If you're going to craft a marvelous blog post, you want to make sure it naturally leads the delighted readers to take a next step.

That next step could be anything.

It could be joining an email newsletter in exchange for a free PDF ebook or guide. It could be filling out an application form. It could be downloading a free checklist that walks the reader through the steps he just read about.

There just needs to be a logical next step for the readers to take, and if you have that next step in mind, you can craft your blog post angle in a way that makes it easy for the readers to take it.

5. **How is this different from anything else out there?**

Remember, any idea that's made it this far in the process should be a unique contribution to the online conversation. You know this. I know this. But your readers may not figure this out until they're halfway through your post.

The last element we need to factor into your angle is the unique value of this post. You need to start thinking about how you would position this piece in context of all the other pieces on the subject out there. Why should it stand out?

Remember, most of your posts are going to be found in two places: social media and search engine searches. But when your posts show up on Facebook or Twitter, they're not appearing in a vacuum. Your blog posts are somewhere in the never-ending scrollathon of photos, videos, links, and witty remarks. How will they stand out? And as for search engines, they aren't returning your blog post as the only option to curious question-askers, either. If your blog post ranks for a search term, it's not ranking alone. Google will present your post alongside nine more posts on the topic—and unless your post is number one, you'll need to give people a really good reason to click on your article. What is that reason?

Make a list of the things your blog post idea has that nobody else has.

Now, this process has been fun, but it's time to choose your angle.

How to turn these into an angle

If you walk through these past few questions on every blog post, you'll find that by this point, you may have already come up with an angle nobody could ever resist: an angle that grabs your readers by the eyeballs and doesn't let go until they've read every word you've written. (I guess that sounds a little rough, but if you ever come up with an angle like that, you'll know that it's a very, very good thing!)

But most of the time, you'll want to work through these questions and start coming up with several angle ideas. You already vetted the post idea's current and potential demand, so you know that people are already likely to want to read a post like this. And you've already looked at a few reasons why:

- You know the specific questions and problems this piece will address.

- You know why people will take the article seriously.

- You know why people will want to share the post.

- You know what people will (or at least should) want to do after reading the post.

Now comes the great game of mix 'n' match: take the answers to the last four questions and use them to answer this one: **What's the #1 thing people will gain from reading this post?**

That's your angle.

Now you know how you're going to write a post that attracts and engages human beings, but there's another important audience to please. We need to discuss how to make a very human-friendly blog post appeal to the ones who are making the judgment calls on what people find when they take their questions to search engines.

We've talked about the humans. Now it's time to talk about the robots.

11

PLANNING FOR ROBOTS

As I write this book, I'm nearing the 25,000 word count mark. That's a lot of talk about blogging, internet marketing, digital customer acquisition, and the like. And if you're used to reading this kind of material, you've probably noticed that I've left one very important, very often-thrown-around term out of this book thus far.

It's SEO.

Go ahead and search the book. I haven't said SEO once.

There are a few reasons for this. For one, this is a book about how to plan effective blog posts, something that involves a lot of SEO best practices but doesn't necessitate me using the term. Another reason is that "SEO" has long been seen as a trade for nerds and crooks. SEO is either seen as a way to trick the search engines into thinking your content is more important than it really is, or it's seen as an almost magic-like skill that only the techiest of minds can master.

But the real reason I've held off on the term SEO is this: everyone has a different idea of what SEO is, and it's a lot easier to address it after we've covered a lot of ground together. To some people, SEO is a scrappy practice of bringing in more online traffic for less money. To others, SEO is about buying as many pay-per-click ads as you can to make sure you're showing up when people search for certain keywords. To others, SEO is a mystery—in fact, I've had clients tell me that they've paid a lot of money for "SEO," and they still have no idea what they accomplished.

It's a strange, touchy subject, and the conversation is always changing.

Just in case you're not familiar with search engine optimization, here's the basics of what you need to know for the sake of this book:

• People look for stuff on search engines (Google, Bing, Yahoo, etc.)

• Search engines give those people a long list of results.

• SEO is a diverse set of practices that put your website toward the top of that list.

It's that simple. And if you've been taking the philosophy I've laid out in this book to heart, then you're already set up to write posts that are optimized for search engines.

However, most of our blog post planning has been with humans in mind. We've dealt with how to come up with ideas, how to vet those ideas, and how to articulate the reasons people should read the resulting posts. But we haven't dealt with some of the more technical aspects of blogging … well, not until now.

Don't worry: I'm not going to spell out all the technical ways to make your website look good to the Googlebots. That's beyond the scope of this book. But we should go over a handful of technical things to consider as you plan your blog post, specifically, word count, imagery, and backlinks. If you start thinking about these three areas before you start writing a post, you'll be well set up to create a piece of content that not only resonates with your human readers, but also gets along with the search engine robots.

We won't get into the nitty-gritty details of technical SEO right now. Now's probably a good time to let you know I'm working on another book specifically about how to write epic blog posts. We'll cover all the juicy details in that book. But for the purposes of planning blog content, there are a few technical things to keep in mind.

Word count

You're not going to like this one.

A lot of very popular bloggers only write posts about 300–600 words long, and for good reason: they want to write bite-sized tidbits of material that people can quickly digest and share. It's understandable that most people blog this way. Anyone can write 300 words on something, and anyone can read 300 words on something. It's easy to commit to writing multiple blog posts a week if you're only cranking out a few hundred words for every piece. In fact, at that rate, a fast writer could write a month's worth of posts in a day!

But I have some bad news for you: Short blog posts aren't a long-term solution when it comes to search engines. Neil Patel ran one of my favorite SEO articles to date back in 2012 on how content length affects ranking and conversion. Here's what he found:

1. The top 10 results for most keywords are at least 2,000 words long.

2. Longer content gets more backlinks.

3. Neil's longer content (>1,500 words) got 68.1% more tweets and 22.6% more Facebook likes than his shorter posts.

4. Longer content gives you a better shot at ranking for long-tail keywords.

5. Longer content converts better, too.

It's not always the case, but long, rich, meaty content tends to win. You'll have a hard time if you try to satisfactorily address a pressing question or challenge in just 500 words!

You probably see where I'm going with this. If you want a lot of search engine traffic in the long run, you'll need to write long content. That may be a bothersome fact to deal with, but I think if we're honest with ourselves, we know this is actually really good news. Why would Google default to a shallow article if there's a more thorough, more well-thought-through, more helpful option?

I like to think of it as a challenge. Google's algorithms favor longer (thorough) content: and that motivates me to write that kind of material. When I sit down to write a blog post, I shoot for a minimum of 2,000 words. It's hard work, but it's thrilling work.

So, how does this affect planning?

Make time to write long, well-researched posts. When you're crafting an outline (which we'll address here shortly), don't be afraid to tease out subpoints and sub-subpoints. Don't be afraid to block out four hours to write a post—especially if the vetting stage has proven that there are a great deal of searches related to your blog post topic.

I've started with the news that's hardest to deliver: your blog posts should be a lot longer than what most people expect. But I promise, there's more to SEO than just getting your hopes for lots of easy traffic dashed! Let's look at another consideration we need to make for our search-engine robot friends: backlinks.

Backlinks

This is a really simple one: before you ever start writing your blog post, you want to have some potential backlinks in mind.

"Hold up, Jeffrey. What's a backlink?"

This is one of those terms that gets thrown around so much in the online marketing world that the people trying to learn the ropes just smile, nod, and try to figure it out later on. A backlink is simply the name for when another site links to your Web page. That's it.

Great content on its own takes a very long time to climb the Google rankings. That's why bloggers like to speed up the process by getting backlinks: links from other sites that say, "Hey, this page is really legit, and you should check it out."

For example: let's say you wrote the end-all article on the different types of coats. It's authoritative, it's well-written, and it explains the nuances in ways that make it easy for even the most basic coat wearers to understand the difference between a sportcoat and a blazer. (Seriously, it's all in the buttons, people!) This is the greatest article on coat types in your language, and when you hit "Publish," you know that there's nothing better on the subject than what you've written.

You could wait for it to rank on its own for searches like, "blazer vs. sportcoat," but that would take a while. Instead, you get Jos. A. Bank, Men's Warehouse, and J. Crew to link to your article. This sends a message to the search engines: "Hey, this post on sportcoats and blazers is so authoritative, the authorities on menswear recommend it to their readers." And the search engines think, "Well, if it's good enough for those guys to recommend, we should probably recommend it, too."

That will help your post rank a lot more quickly.

Why? Because the search engines are in business to do one thing: serve up the most helpful content they can to curious users of the Internet. Think about it: if you kept Googling things like "sportcoat vs. blazer" or "Free will vs. Calvinism" and didn't find helpful articles, what would you do? You'd stop using Google!

That's why search engines pay attention to the links you get from authoritative sites. They want to make sure that if someone important online has found a very, very helpful article, they start serving it up to people asking the questions that article answers.

What does this have to do with planning? When you're planning a blog post, you need to have a good idea of the websites you want to get backlinks from. Make a list of sites you would love to get a mention from, and plan your post accordingly. This will help you when you start writing the post, because you'll already have a list of sites to court for links in mind, and you'll craft your content in such a way that will make it easy for those sites to share it.

Now, we've looked at how long you should plan a post to be, and we've touched on the importance of having a list of prospective backlinks to keep in mind when you write. We need to cover one more important part of the process: targeting keywords for search engines to associate with your article.

Target concepts

For the majority of search engine history, the way you got to the top of search results was by targeting keywords. If you've ever had a conversation with an SEO professional, you've heard the term "keyword" a few hundred times already, but just so we're all on the same page: a keyword is any word or phrase that you want search engines to associate with your Web page.

For example, if you ran a software company that specialized in growing an email list, some keywords you would want to target may be "lead generation," "how to get email subscribers," and "subject line best practices."

This is just as true today as it was ten years ago, but the ways search engines associate web pages with keywords has changed a lot over the years.

If it were 2002 and you wanted to show up at the top of the pile when people Googled "email marketing," you would simply make sure a page on your website said "email marketing" a lot. You'd only need about 300 words, and you'd put "email marketing" in a few choice places in the code of your site as well as in the words that appear on the page. This would work because search engines would see this page and think, "Wow! This page says 'email marketing' a lot. It must be all about email marketing—we'd better recommend this site to people searching for email marketing stuff!" In other words, it was kind of easy. The common practice was to target the keywords you wanted to be associated with, wrote a page that mentioned those keywords over and over again, and *voila!* you ranked for those keywords.

That's not how it works today. In fact, if you tried to do this, you'd actually get penalized!

"Why? What changed?"

Well, Internet marketers gamed the system (and they got really, really rich). You could find terrible, unhelpful, useless, nonsensical articles on the first page of Google results—pages that got there simply because someone thought, "Hey, this is easy enough. Let's throw as many awesome keywords into this page as possible so it ranks really high!" This practice is called "keyword stuffing," and as you can imagine, it's not viewed very favorably in today's world of marketers.

Those tactics won in the short-term. But the folks doing this forgot something very important: Google, Microsoft, and Yahoo are for-profit software companies, and a for-profit software company needs to please their users.

Remember: we use search engines because we can depend on them to recommend content that's relevant to our searches. If Google kept serving up low-quality articles, what would we do? We'd stop using Google! And that would be pretty bad for Google.

So the search engines update their algorithms every now and again to make sure they're giving searchers like us (and your prospective customers) the best content they can. That's good for you, and not as good for the people who have capitalized off those old keyword-stuffing tactics.

Why is it good for you? Because Google and the other search engines have only become smarter. They're not just looking at the exact words people are typing; they're checking those words against other search terms to see what you're *really* looking for. And what you're really looking for has more to do with concept than with specific keywords.

For example, let's say you're visiting my home town of Wake Forest, North Carolina for a weekend, and you want to find a great deli there. You might Google "best sandwich in Wake Forest." You're looking for a deli, but you searched for sandwiches—not a bad search. Google's not going to penalize you for looking up "sandwiches" instead of "deli," and they'll still recommend Over the Falls Deli to you.

That's because the folks at Google aren't just searching for the words you typed. They're looking for the words related to the words you type.

This is why I recommend a departure from the traditional SEO advice. Instead of targeting keywords, target concepts. You don't want to spend all your time trying to gain traffic for a certain phrase when you could own all the traffic for all the related phrases!

So, before you sit down to write a blog post, make sure you've thought through the concept in its entirety. Think of all the possible questions someone might have that your post idea might answer—and answer them! This will help you show up in Google, Bing, and Yahoo when people search for the answers to questions related to your blog post idea.

Why am I bringing this up in a book on planning blog posts? Because you want to get the most mileage out of every post you write, and it's more efficient to write one post that ranks for 10 very closely related keywords than 10 posts that rank for each one of those keywords!

Now that we've talked about planning for people and planning for robots, there's one more important area that we need to talk about before we dive into the mechanics of crafting the perfect blog post outline: planning for promotion.

12

PLANNING FOR PROMOTION

This is a short one, but an important one. In fact, I feel like understanding this step was a turning point for me in my marketing career.

When people hear the word, "promotion," they often think "buying other people's attention." That means promotion, as a concept, doesn't have the best reputation. Most people don't like being on the receiving end of banner ads, billboards, TV commercials, and those guys spinning signs on the corners of busy intersections. But paid promotion is really just a subset of promotion as a whole. And promotion as a whole can make or break your blog post's success.

Promotion is important because, before you even start writing your post, you should have a general idea of how people are going to get to it. Any blog post is going to get two kinds of traffic: the kind you as a blogger can influence, and the kind you can't. Promotion is managing the kind of traffic you can influence.

That means promotion can entail all kinds of approaches to getting people to your blog post, some paid, and some free. Here are a few ways you can go about promoting a blog post:

- Emailing your email list with news about your latest blog post
- Sharing your post to your own social networks
- Search engine advertising
- Social media advertising
- Asking influencers to share your content on social media
- Asking influencers to link to your content from their blogs
- Reaching out to reporters and news publications with a story

And of course, that's far from an exhaustive list.

The concept of promotion may leave a bad taste in your mouth, especially if it's in the context of promoting yourself. I wasn't always a fan of it, myself. I thought, "If this content is good enough, people will find it and share it. Besides, wouldn't it look tacky if I were just tooting my own horn about this blog post I wrote?"

That was my outlook for about the first year that I blogged. I was slaving away over a computer keyboard trying to crank out excellent content, but not bothering to try to direct people to it (outside of my Facebook and Twitter friends). I was spinning my wheels, just because I didn't want to be a self-promoting blowhard.

But then I wondered, "If I write all this content, hit 'Publish,' and don't tell anyone, how are people supposed to find it?" They won't. It's a tree-falling-in-an-empty-forest situation.

That was my first mistake: thinking I didn't need to promote my content.

Things got a little bit better after that. I would write blog posts and design infographics, and then reach out to prominent bloggers asking them to share it. I was also building an email list to disseminate the news of new blog posts too.

This lead to an increase in traffic—actually a huge increase. But I ran into another problem: not all of my posts were getting shared. Not all of them were interesting to these big-time bloggers I was getting backlinks from. Some of these posts ranked well in the search engines, and some didn't.

That's because I had moved from one mistake to another. Whereas before I was writing blog posts and not bothering to drive traffic to them, now I was writing blog posts and then, only after the post was already done, would I try to promote them. I would find myself looking at a completed post and asking myself, "OK, now … how am I going to get people to read this?"

You can see where I'm going with this. Even the very best of blog posts won't see any results without a degree of promotion, so it's better to take promotion into account before you start writing than it is to write an incredibly informative blog post and then have to deal with the problem of getting people to read it! It's better to have a plan for promotion in place before you ever start writing. This way, as you're crafting the content, you have a decent idea of where the readers are coming from. You can craft your content in such a way that it makes perfect sense to the readers coming from the sources you have in mind. You can write the post with a few key influencers in mind—people you would like to get backlinks from once the post is published. The better you know how people will be getting to your content, the better prepared you will be to write the content that satisfies them.

So, how do you plan for promotion? In the last section, you created a list of websites you would want to get a backlink from. This is a good start. Now, it's time to answer these questions:

How will people get to this blog post? Answers will probably be a mix of social shares, organic search traffic, referrals from other websites, and perhaps some paid promotion.

How do I tap into the post idea's current and potential demand? You've already assessed the post idea's demand in the vetting process. It's time to start thinking of how to position this post in a way that taps into that demand. What sort of images will you use? What words should the headline include? When should this post go live?

How can I write this post in a way that will make influencers want to share it and link to it? You want to write posts that make influencers look good. Cite them as sources, and they'll be far more likely to tell others about it. Here's an excerpt on the matter from an article I wrote:

> When you're writing content, sprinkle in some nods to the people your target audience respects. That might look like pointing to their work as a case study. It might look like linking to one of their blog posts for more information. It might look like giving them a direct shout out and linking to their Twitter handle.
>
> Doing this gives you a few benefits. First, it helps bring on the warm fuzzies for those experts. Second, if you recognize the people your audience respects, you make it easier for them to take you seriously.

Sidenote: this happens to all of us. We immediately feel more connected to people who root for the same sports teams, listen to the same bands, and chow down at the same favorite restaurants. It works the same way with experts. If I know you read my favorite blog, I'm more likely to think you know what you're talking about.

Could I help more people by paying to promote this content? You can always buy a few hundred dollars' worth of Facebook or Google pay-per-click ads to drive more traffic. And paying for traffic can be very helpful—you can drive more traffic to a page right away instead of waiting for it to rank on its own in the search engines. You just need to ask yourself if it's worth the advertising price.

Moving on

If you've answered these questions, then, congrats: it's time to move on to the climax of this book. We're going to look at how to build an outline for your blog post!

13

HOW TO OUTLINE A BLOG POST

Almost done!

You've generated a blog post idea.

You've vetted it, so you know it's good.

You've thought through why it will appeal to people and robots, and you know how those people are going to find it.

Now comes my favorite part. Now, we take everything we know about this blog post idea and formulate a thorough outline. We'll turn all the different ways we've explored and teased and analyzed this blog post idea into a structured, intuitive flow for the final post. The rest of this chapter will be about how to outline a blog post—or more accurately, how to make incredible, actionable outlines that make life easier for you, your readers, and any writers you'll hire.

The word "outline" is pretty straightforward, but it's probably worth defining up front. When I say "outline," I'm not referring to a simple ordered list of points bookended by the words "Introduction" and "Conclusion." Neither am I talking about a blog post's table of contents. These approaches work just fine for students writing essays, but when you're writing authoritative content, you need more than just a three-point structure. You need a plan—a plan to hold the reader's hand through the process of asking a question and discovering the answer.

Your outline is more than an outline: it's a strategy for drawing readers in, teaching them what they want to learn, and making sure that every paragraph builds on top of the last and leads seamlessly into the next. That means we're not just going to look at structuring the points of a blog post. We're going to look at headlines, section headings, transitions, citations, images, and your call to action at the end.

That may sound like a lot of work for an outline. After all, if you've already vetted the idea and gone through the process of figuring out why other people are going to care about it, shouldn't you be able to just jump in and start writing?

Ideally, that's what would happen. However, we're not ideal bloggers in an ideal blogging world. We have distractions. We have doubts. We have a hard time thinking like other people when we're writing.

But outlines (thorough, strategic outlines) give us the upper hand. In fact, a solid outline can give you four significant advantages when it comes to blogging.

1. Outlines make blog posts easier to write

A good outline structures your thoughts so well that when you sit down to write, all you're doing is sitting down to write. Remember the locomotive vs. ATV analogy from earlier? We want to lay down the tracks so that we can move 15,000 tons of high-quality content from our brains to the page. An outline helps us do that, because we're not hemming and hawing over what comes next or what should have come earlier. That means less of our time gets caught up in rethinking our words and more goes into making them.

2. Outlines make blog posts easier to finish

I often struggle with ending a blog post. I get to a point where I think, "I've come this far; but I could expand this even further!" It ends up with me taking much longer to finish a blog post than I originally planned, all because I had scope creep.

But I've found that a good outline can help me overcome this problem (and infuse a few more hours into my week). If I've written down a thorough plan for the blog post, a plan with a clear beginning, middle, and destination, then I don't need to worry about filling it in later. I can rest assured that when I reach the end of the post, I've reached the end of the post. Granted, there will be some editing, but for the most part, I'm done.

3. Outlines make blog posts easier to read

This one is pretty straightforward. A well-structured post is a lot easier to follow than a poorly-structured post. That means your readers are more likely to read the whole post—which is good for two big reasons. Firstly, if your readers are consuming the whole post, you're probably helping them more than you would if your article was just something they quickly skimmed.

Secondly, if people are reading the whole post, they're spending a lot more time on your site than they would be if they were just sampling your section headers. Without getting into too much technical detail, the more time people spend on your site, the more search engines will favor your pages in their results. This is because search engines assume that, people tend to spend more time on helpful, satisfying pages than they do on frustrating, unhelpful pages.

On top of all this, a strong outline makes your post easier for your readers to remember. The better they retain the information you lay out, the more likely they are to recommend your post to others.

4. Outlines make blog posts easier to outsource and collaborate on

While most bloggers come up with their own ideas and then execute on them, there's a good chance that, if you're reading this book, you may not actually be the only person writing the blog posts for your organization. You may be the communications manager, or the director of marketing, or even an executive. Coming up with the strategic direction is your job; most of the execution will fall to someone else.

An outline makes it easier to hand off those ideas to someone else.

For example, imagine you were running a website promoting homes for sale in Washington State. You know it would help to write the authoritative blog post on the best neighborhoods in Seattle. But you don't have time to write such a post—why, 2,500 words may not even do it justice!

So you send an email to your in-house marketing person saying, "I'd like to rank in the top three search engine results for searches surrounding places to live in Seattle. Please write a blog post on the topic."

Now, what is your marketing team going to give you? You don't know, and neither do they! If you had an SEO and content marketing expert on the team who knew a decent amount about Seattle neighborhoods (or could research the topic well), then you'd be in luck. But do you (or your marketing agency) have such a person on the team? Not everyone does.

I find that this leads to the client (be it you or your boss) and the author (be it you, your marketing team, or your freelancers) into a cycle of frustration. The client has an idea in their head. The author takes a stab at the article based on what they're given. The first draft the client sees isn't what they had in mind, so they tell the author to change a few things. The author does so, but by clearing up the first round of mistakes, they've made it easier to spot other ways the article just doesn't line up with the client's vision. This leads to more revisions and more critiques until the final published blog post is something both parties are sick of seeing.

An outline alleviates that pain. If you're the client, you can write up a detailed outline that specifies to the author exactly what you want. If you're the author (and the client didn't give you an outline), before you ever start writing a post, you can write up a detailed outline based on the client's request. An outline sets expectations ahead of time, and it's a lot quicker to make than an entire blog post. You can tweak an outline all you like, and then once it's set, it's set.

That means fewer revisions and more productivity.

You get it: outlines save lots of time and frustration, and lead to more productivity when it comes to writing blog posts. Outlines are the tracks we lay down for the locomotives of our minds.

You ready to start laying some track? Me, too. Let's go!

The anatomy of a good outline

(First off, that section header is kind of funny to me. It's almost like writing, "the anatomy of a good anatomy." But I digress.)

A good outline will cover seven basic parts of a blog post:

1. Working headline

2. Purpose

3. Section headers (or "subheaders")

4. Transitions

5. Images

6. Sources

7. Call to action (or "CTA")

Let's walk through each of these, and how to address them in your outline.

Working headline

If you've been in the copywriting business for more than a few months, this step scares the living daylights out of you. You already know that headlines are the single most important piece of an article. You've heard that you should spend as much as 50% of your writing time on your headline. (I don't believe that's true, but that's another book for another day.)

There's a lot of hype around headlines, and there's a good reason for that. Advertising legend David Oglivy famously wrote in *Confessions of an Advertising Man* that "On the average, five times as many people read the headline as read the body copy. When you have written your headline, you have spent eighty cents out of your dollar."

That's a little bit of pressure, and that's why anyone reading this with copywriting experience should be a little scared of including a headline in an outline. After all, your headline is your first, best, and sometimes only shot at grabbing someone's attention. It deserves a lot of attention.

However, we're not talking about the final headline yet: we just need a working headline. You will want to begin your outline with a title that states the main reason people should want to read your article. It could be as simple as "How to get a Bible college scholarship in Missouri." It's more important that you can solidify the idea behind your post than it is that you can craft the ultimate headline—at least at this point in the game.

Once you have a working headline, it will be easier to outline your post. And once your post is outlined, it will be easier to refine your working headline into a compelling, eyeball-attracting work of marketing art.

Here are a few tips to keep in mind while you're writing a working headline:

1. Blog posts aren't books, and headlines aren't titles.

It's tempting to begin your blog post with a title that makes it sound like a work of art. For example, if a transplant from the South were to write a blog post on how to cope with homesickness, they might want to title it, "Longing for the Smokies." That might be an artistic title for a short story, or an essay, or a poem. But if you're trying to write a helpful blog post on how to deal with homesickness, you'll want to be more straightforward.

That's because headlines are more than titles. They're your shot at getting someone who's scrolling through their Facebook news feed to click through. They're the reason people will click through to your article from search engines. That means a headline's utility is more important than its cleverness.

In other words, your headline isn't a title for your idea—your headline is the hook for your idea. Your headline should pitch the main benefit of your blog post so well that anyone in your target audience is going to want to read more.

So, when you're writing up your working headline, ask yourself, "Does this pitch the main reason anyone would read this article?" Remember our work a few sections ago on why this blog post idea is going to be appealing to your readers. You'll want to write a working headline that gets across the bulk of the message.

2. Include some of your SEO concepts.

From a search engine perspective, it doesn't hurt to include some of the more highly searched keywords in your headline. You don't necessarily need to use one exact phrase in your headline—search engines are smart enough to take note of root words and related terms. The important thing is that your headline reflects those target concepts you thought through in the "planning for robots" section earlier.

For example, if I wanted to write a post that ranked #1 for search terms like, "progressive seminaries," my working headline would probably be something like, "The 10 most progressive seminaries, and why." I'd definitely want to work on this some more after writing the post, but this gives me a good start.

3. Set credible expectations that you can deliver on.

You may be familiar with the term "clickbait." It's a controversial practice in the blogging world. Clickbaiters write headlines and use images with the sole purpose of arousing impulsive curiosity—which can only be satisfied by clicking on a link to the content being promoted.

You've seen clickbait. You know those annoying ads at the bottom of news sites telling you to read up on the latest celebrity gossip, find out how to get a good deal on cruise cabins, learn which foods not to eat, or how to look 25 years younger using one unbelievable trick? That's clickbait.

What does that have to do with your blog outline?

You don't want to sound like that.

You want a headline that makes a promise you can deliver on. You want a headline that immediately establishes your content as credible and helpful.

Credible and helpful—those may be the most important qualities of a blog post headline. You need a headline that's credible, otherwise people won't take you seriously. For example, a blog post titled, "The secret trick to doubling your salary in six months" isn't very credible. You're making a vague promise that any savvy reader knows you can't (consistently) keep. The same post entitled "How to get bigger raises, and more often." is a little more believable.

Likewise, a post titled, "Meet Dr. Jones, our archaeology department chair" is very credible, but not very helpful. Why should someone be interested in Dr. Jones? But "The man who found the Holy Grail … and teaches classes at WWU" … that's interesting! Anyone interested in archaeology would find a blog post about this man to be helpful.

So, as you write your working headline, remember that your headline is a promise to your future readers. Make the promise good. Make it believable. Make it helpful. And make sure you can deliver.

4. Keep it simple.

You'll refine this headline later on: it's just important that your headline aligns with the angle of this post. Try to keep it under 10 words for now. Don't overthink it. The important thing is that you set yourself up for an easy-to-write post, and a rough headline helps you outline such a post without constantly changing direction.

Now that you have a working headline, it's time to move on to the next crucial piece of your outline: the blog post purpose statements.

Blog post purpose

Your working headline is a rough summary of why your audience will want to read this post. Now you need to balance that with a rough summary of why you want to write the post.

I find that this is easier to pull off when you're answering a set of three questions.

1. What do you want to accomplish with this post?

Your answer should be straightforward, simple, and sensible—in other words, it needs to be an answer you would readily give your boss if he or she asks! A possible answer could be, "To rank on the first page of organic search results for 'aquariums near Atlanta,'" or, "To broaden our brand's perceived authority on auto safety."

Whatever your answer is, it needs to make sense to your organization. (And it should be something that this post can actually accomplish.)

2. How does this fit into the bigger picture?

Odds are you're not just writing one blog post this year. How will this post fit into your overall blogging strategy? How does the answer to the first question help the organization as a whole?

You don't need to go into intense detail on this. A simple sentence like, "The call to action will generate relevant leads for our sales department" can do the trick nicely. Stating the way this post fits into your overall strategy will help you focus when you're writing the post.

3. Are there any targeted search concepts?

Not every post will be planned to generate long-term organic traffic from search engines. However, you will want to have some idea of what kinds of searches you'd like this post to be a result for. Include your targeted search concepts here (which you will have already established if you planned for robots in the previous section of this chapter).

This step is especially important if you're writing an outline to pass off to another author. Giving them this target will help them include those key phrases in paragraphs and subheaders throughout the post.

Now, write down these answers after the headline in your outline. I like to have a bulleted list:

- **Purpose:** [Answer]

- **Context:** [Answer]

- **Target concepts and keywords:** [List]

If you couple this little bit of information with your working headline, you have a two-part foundation for your blog post outline. You know why people want to read it, and you know why you should write it.

Now it's time to start building the skeleton of the blog post itself.

Section headers

I don't know about you, but I tend to get some sort of writing paralysis when I don't know where I'm going. Left to my own devices, I could stew and stew over a 100-word paragraph for 30 minutes if I don't know what the paragraph is leading into.

Not everyone is like me. Some people love the blank white page: they can have an idea, sit down, and pen 1,600 words in an hour without any outline or direction. The idea is enough for them.

But for me (and most people), writing doesn't work like this. We need some sort of structure: a roadmap telling us how far we've come, where we're going, and how long it takes to get there.

That's where your section headers come in. In this part of your outline, you'll lay out the basic sections of your blog post.

Now, some of you are probably pretty confident when it comes to writing outlines. You still remember needing to outline your essays in college, outline your speeches at business presentations, and even outline conversation points for family functions. You probably know 95% of what I'm going to cover in the next few hundred words or so. If you feel like you know your way around an outline just fine, feel free to skip to the next section, "Images." But if you'd like to know specifically how to structure your blog posts so that they're both easy to write and easy to read online (which is that extra 5%), stay with me here.

When it comes to writing outlines, it's helpful to remember that every good blog post should resemble both a movie and a conversation.

A blog post resembles a movie in that it should have a clear beginning, middle, and end. The beginning should lay out the challenges that need to be overcome. The middle should be the events that ensue when you're trying to solve those challenges. The end is when the challenge is resolved.

In the same way, the sections of your blog posts should have a clear beginning, middle, and end. A blog post beginning will generally accomplish three essential things:

- Connect the headline to the content.

- Set up the reader's problem, challenge, or question.

- Give a brief overview of how the post will help the reader with that problem, challenge, or question.

Sometimes the beginning of a blog post won't need any special section headers. In fact, sometimes all you need for your introduction is a few simple sentences to unpack the headline. After that, it's all about the middle section.

Middle sections, on the other hand, aren't so easy.

You need to structure out your subheaders in a way that tell the general story of your post. That means you'll lay out the sections of your post so that each piece builds on the last and leads into the next.

What should those section headers be? That's for you to decide. There are a number of ways to go with these. You could make a list. You could write each subheader as the title of a miniature post within your blog. You could make the subheaders general and straightforward. You could arrange them into clever acrostics.

You can do whatever you want, so long as the information flow is consistent and easy to follow. (And of course, from an SEO standpoint, it doesn't hurt to sprinkle those target keywords throughout your headers!)

As to the blog-post movie's end, we'll cover this soon (in the "Call to action" section).

A good blog post is like a good movie in that it has a clear beginning, middle, and end. If you've mapped out your subheaders, you're only about halfway through this part of the outline-building process. The next part is even more important.

A good blog post is also like a conversation, in that it doesn't just talk at the reader—it thinks through the issues with the reader. It answers questions the reader has. It invites feedback. It doesn't feel canned.

This is the other piece you need to account for when you're laying out the sections of your outline: what are the questions your article will raise in the reader's mind? How will you answer them, and where in the piece will you answer them?

Once you've written out your section headers, think through the content that you'll be writing beneath each of these. What questions will be jumping into your reader's mind? What unknown concepts are you introducing? What will need case studies and illustrations?

Take note of these, and then mark under your subheaders which questions will come up, and where in the article you will address them. This will keep you mindful of your readers when you sit down to write.

This step may sound like a pain, but you need to know that this is the defining difference between a good blog post and a legendary blog post. A good blog post lays out the information in an easy-to-understand way. A legendary blog post lays information out in such a way that the readers don't even realize they're learning. Every question that comes to mind is anticipated. Every concern is addressed.

It takes a lot of empathy to write those kinds of posts. (It also takes a lot of work!) But you can do it.

Go multiple layers deep. When I started writing blog outlines, I just wrote down the major points I needed to cover. But then when it came time for me to write the posts themselves, I would get hung up on how to get started on one section. I needed to either wrack my brain for the thoughts I had wanted to convey at the time I wrote the outline, or just start over. Sometimes I'd throw the entire section idea out.

That's because my outlines needed more detail—a great deal more detail. A useful outline isn't just a collection of points. It's a collection of points, and subpoints, and sub-subpoints. A useful outline structures everything you want to say. A useful outline is so detailed that you (or whomever you get to write this blog post) cannot possibly sit down and think, "What do I say now?"

"Woah, Jeffrey. Isn't the point of an outline to give a general overview of what I need to cover?"

No! Nobody is going to read your outline except you and whomever you're paying to write this post. I'll say that again: Nobody is going to read your outline except you. Your outline isn't giving you a general overview. Your outline is your detailed, step-by-step instructions to your future self on how this blog post should be written.

That means you don't want to waste your time writing an outline that doesn't do its job. When you write an outline, you craft something so thoughtful, so comprehensive, that you can sit down to write the post without ever, ever needing to think about what you'll say next.

So, how detailed is detailed enough?

To me (and this is just me) the ideal outline would have one point per paragraph. You do not need to get that detailed if you don't want. I just know that it's a lot easier for me to think through the flow of an article when I'm thinking of the article as a whole than it is to think up something to write next when I'm in the middle of writing a piece.

You may not need that kind of detail, and that's OK. You just need to structure your subheaders specifically enough for you to know exactly what you want to write when the time comes to write.

Structuring your subheaders isn't always easy. But there are some shortcuts! Start with list-style blog posts ("The 10 best cars for families on a $5,000 budget"). These almost come pre-structured, so you get to focus on arranging the pieces rather than coming up with the pieces yourself. Another quick win is to write how-to articles. These are similar to lists in that they cover a process, which has a built-in structure, and they give you some practice in anticipating questions the reader may have. (For example, "What if I don't have a ____?")

Once you've written the section headers for your blog post, the rest is smooth sailing. Now we just need to talk about a few "gotchas" to look out for in your blog outlines.

Transitions

This one's a simple add-on to your subheaders. You don't want to be caught in a spot where you've finished up one section but you're not sure how to move on to the next; therefore, it's helpful to give yourself a few throwaway lines between your sections to link them together.

You'll see those throughout a lot of my blog posts (and in this book): I'll say something like, "Now you know X, but X won't really do you any good without Y. So let's talk about Y."

This will help you as you write, because as you draw each section to a close, you'll find that you've already given yourself a springboard into the next section!

Images

Most of your outline will be focused on text, because that's going to make up the majority of your post. However, you also want to start planning out your imagery in the pre-writing stages. Imagery is an important part of your blog post strategy for a few reasons.

Images can be an effective way to break up very long articles. If you're dealing with a lot of heady content, it helps to give your readers something visual to complement all the text they're drinking in. Images can also help you make complex ideas, arguments, and arrangements easier to understand. For example, if you wanted to make a list of the hottest tech startups in Boston, it may help your readers to give them a visual map of the city that illustrates your findings.

Beyond their use as visual and reading aides, images can help your blog post gain more attention on social media. A blog post with at least one image is going to perform better on social media than it would without an image. You've probably noticed that when one of your friends shares a link to an article or website on Facebook or Twitter, you see an image accompanying the text and link. And it's probably no surprise to you that people tend to click on posts with images a lot more than they click on regular old links.

Look at the subpoints and transitions you've written down. Would any of your blog post's sections benefit from some visuals? What about the overall concept of the blog post—does it merit an infographic or poster to make the entirety of the post easier to remember?

Write down the kinds of images your blog post will need (and where in the blog post they should go) in your outline.

Sources

By this point, you will have already made a list of a few key sources you plan to cite in your blog post. Go over your outline again, this time looking for the best places in the article to bring up those killer quotes and case studies.

Next steps (call to action)

If you've followed the steps in this guide, you have a rather detailed outline for every part of your blog post except the ending. This is intentional, because your blog post's ending shouldn't ever be a simple stop. Remember, you're blogging to attract new people in your target audience and keep your existing audience engaged—that means you can't just stop with a fine blog post. You need to give your readers something to do next.

You could call this the end of your blog post. You could also call this the beginning of a very awesome new relationship with your new readers. You could also consider this just another midway point in a potential customer's journey to finding a solution (which may or may not be yours).

No matter how you slice it, each blog post should offer a logical, helpful next step to the reader. What will yours be?

It could be something simple, like, "Want to know more about our product? Click here to request more information." It could be more involved, like, "Did you enjoy this article on the top 10 state parks in the Southwest? Download our whitepaper on the top national parks in the country."

Your call to action could be anything, but no matter what it is, you'll want to keep a few principles in mind.

1. Make sure it relates to the content people are already reading. If someone has just read an article on the benefits of honeymooning in Texas, make sure the next step you propose has something to do with either honeymoons or Texas. This helps you in a few ways. For one, you'll see more people taking the actions you want them to take on your blog. Another way you'll benefit from this is that you'll be engaging people who are more likely to appreciate your offerings—if you're blogging in ways that benefit both you and the reader, then a relevant call to action will boost your chances of gaining more warm leads in your target niche.

2. Make it worth the reader's while. Your call to action could be as simple as clicking a link, but most calls to action in the business world involve capturing someone's contact information.

However, if you're going to ask for the reader's private information (email address, name, company, etc.), you'll need to offer something valuable enough for them to want to give you that information. The more valuable the thing you're offering, the more people will be willing to divulge the information you're trying to gather!

3. Keep it simple. We're not going to get into the nitty-gritty details of how to write button text and blog post paragraphs that close the sale on the page. But you should plan your call to action in such a way that the next step makes perfect sense and doesn't involve many steps or hoop-jumpings on the reader's part.

Once you've taken these things into account, write down your call to action at the bottom of your outline.

Congratulations: your outline is done!

You're ready to sit down and hammer this blog post out.

14

WRAPPING UP

You've done it.

You've developed a system for generating blog post ideas. You know how to capture those ideas and then filter them through a vetting system. And you know how to flesh the good ideas out into comprehensive, helpful, outlines.

You've done everything you need to do before you write the next post. I'm very, very happy for you!

And I'm also very grateful to you for reading this guide. It's a bit of a doozy. (You should have seen the monster I was planning to write. I actually had to slice the original book idea down into three different book ideas just so I wouldn't be dropping a 100,000-word e-tome on you!) I appreciate the time that went into reading this, and I believe it will pay off greatly as you plan your own future blog posts.

It will.

You know it will.

Happy blogging, friend.

www.ingramcontent.com/pod-product-compliance
Lightning Source LLC
Chambersburg PA
CBHW062107220526
45471CB00010B/3634